MW00580496

Early Praise for
Dare to be Fabulous

"This book holds together the power women find when they are honest and courageous and truthful. Some of these stories moved me to tears, others made me believe in humanity again, many I could identify with. This book brought me tremendous joy, insight and brought me back to believe in the human spirit."

~ JULIANNA MARGULIES,
multiple award-winning actor and
author of *Sunshine Girl: An Unexpected Life*

Track the path to your own true north

Every story in this book
is followed by a personal writing prompt

Consider the
Dare to be Fabulous Journal Notebook
as your writing companion

Copyright © 2022 By Johanna McCloy

No part of this book may be reproduced in any form or by any electronic or mechanical means, including photography, recording, or by any information storage and retrieval system or technologies now known or later developed, without permission in writing from the publisher or author, except by reviewers, who may quote brief passages in a review. For permission requests, please contact info@ bordertownpublishing.com

Story Permissions and copyrights are provided in the Acknowledgements.

Publisher's Cataloging in Publication Data

Names: McCloy, Johanna, editor.
Title: Dare to be fabulous : follow the journeys of daring women on the path to finding their true north / edited by Johanna McCloy.
Description: Includes bibliographical references. | Berkeley, CA: Bordertown Publishing, 2022.
Identifiers: ISBN: 978-0-9975963-2-8 (paperback) | 978-9975963-3-5 (ebook)
Subjects: LCSH Women--Biography. | Self-actualization (Psychology) | Success. | Happiness. | Self help. | Essays. | BISAC SELF-HELP / General | SELF-HELP / Motivational & Inspirational | SELF-HELP / Personal Growth / Happiness
Classification: LCC HQ1180 .D37 2022 | DDC 305.4—dc23

Library of Congress Control Number: 2022910553

ISBN 978-0-9975963-2-8 (paperback)
ISBN 978-0-9975963-3-5 (ebook)

Cover by Teddi Black
Interior formatting by Megan McCullough

Printed in the United States of America

Bordertown Publishing
Berkeley, CA
www.bordertownpublishing.com

Follow the journeys of
daring women on the path
to finding their true north

dare
to be
fabulous

EDITED BY
JOHANNA McCLOY

Bordertown
Publishing
Berkeley, California

"A sheltered life can be a daring life as well. For all serious daring starts from within."

~ Eudora Welty

Contents

"My life has been long, and believing that life loves the liver of it, I have dared to try many things, sometimes trembling, but daring still."

~ Maya Angelou

Introduction

Do you dare to be fabulous? Yes! You do. We all do, every single one of us, in our own ways.

You are unique. You were born with a combination of specific genes, into a particular culture, with its own set of values, expectations, and rules. You have navigated a very personal path that led to today. A path carved by outside expectations, personal choices, convention, fear, risk, struggle, love, passion, success, pain, joy . . . and so much more. Talk about unique! No one is you. And you are no one else.

Look around you. Contemplate that truth for every person you see. There are hundreds of circumstances and experiences that help to characterize each individual's path. We're all different, but what we do have in common is as simple and pure and deep as it gets: our humanity. Living a life with feeling.

We can all relate to how it feels when we dare to cross a personal divide, enter unknown terrain, take a chance, shift perspective, face a fear, or stretch a little. Liberating ourselves from long-established routines, behaviors, expectations, or fears, can be very empowering and even provide a healthy dose of levity and laughter.

This is daring to be fabulous. And it's how we find our true north.

Personal stories in this book cover a wide variety of experiences — some funny, some serious, and many in-between — with contributors ranging from well-known activists, musicians, and journalists, to one woman who remains "Alcoholic Anonymous." We're all in this together. The personal is universal, and the universal personal. Every affirming action reverberates into the world and bolsters others in its wake.

Stories in this book were selected from nearly 50 stories previously featured on DaretobeFabulous.com, a website I've hosted and edited since 2010. I selected this collection based on the range of topics and themes they convey. With only three exceptions, all of these stories were written for *Dare to be Fabulous*.

I'm sincere when I say, "You'll laugh! You'll cry!" when reading this collection. Mostly, you'll nod with understanding and hold a continual smile on your face. What's not to like about that?

A prominent quote precedes each story, and a personal prompt follows it. (All story contributors were also invited to suggest a prompt of their own; when they did, it's noted.) My hope with these additional features is to further inspire thought, reflection, imagination, and action. This is why I also created the *Dare to be Fabulous Journal Notebook* as a writing companion. Every feature in this book can serve as a writing prompt. I like how they interrelate in interesting ways. One idea is to select a story each day, and use that quote/story/prompt combination as inspiration for daily writing.

Finally, I should note that this book is also a personal act of daring. I've been talking about publishing a *Dare to be Fabulous* book for years. I even edited and published another book, which is doing well. Why the hesitation on this one? Fear, basically. Concern about judgement or criticism. The amount of work was part of it, but most importantly, I wanted to do right by all my wonderful contributors.

To publish this book, I had to accept that there is no such thing as "perfect" and that mistakes would likely happen, as they do even in mainstream releases (if you see a mistake, please do let me know.) Also, a creative work is never truly "finished," because changes and new ideas continually come to mind, so I just had to let go at some point and accept that what I had would go to publication.

So, daring I've done. And this book is the result of a lot of work, diligence, passion, a heart full of love for all the contributors in this collection, and the desire to share their stories widely.

I hope that the spirit of *Dare to be Fabulous* provides some good fodder for your own journey. May it hone your compass and help you on the path to your own true north.

Johanna McCloy
Editor

"I have bursts of being a lady,
but it doesn't last long."

~ Shelley Winters

Isn't That Fabulous?

Fabulous. It isn't a word that comes naturally to me. To say it right, you really have to draw it out . . . faaaabulous. Saying it feels alien, like smoking a hookah or playing inter-office softball.

Fabulous women have long, carefully tousled hair or extremely short micro-bangs. They wear billowy caftans with "élan." Fabulous women throw casually chic dinners with large artisan bowls of artfully torn bread. They wield their feminine power confidently. They belt their coats.

I am not one of those fabulous women. I've never worn *anything* with élan except maybe that one Halloween in sixth grade, when I went as a Watergate tape. I tell myself to talk less after almost every encounter with anyone. And my torn bread is less artful than it is dismembered.

Don't get me wrong: I'm not self-loathing — except when appropriate. But in no way, shape, or form am I that kind of fabulous. I know, because I tried to be . . . once.

Actually, twice. I did something before the experience I'm about to share, which I thought was fairly fabulous; something I thought was original and witty and cool. However, I've been informed, by most who hear the tale, that eating a beef rib in a stall in the women's bathroom of Harrods so I could say I've done something no one else has done in the 2000 years of London's existence, isn't fabulous. Apparently, it's weird and gross.

Okay. Lesson learned, don't tell that story.

So, in this particular instance, I decided to do something mainstream and stereotypically, undeniably, by-the-book fabulous.

I went topless. Not just topless, mind you, but topless in the south of France — Cannes, no less.

Full on, *Rihanna* fabulous.

I was at the beach in Cannes, and everyone around me was topless. The fact is, I would have stood out if I didn't. Best of all, I knew absolutely no one, and no one knew me, so I was completely anonymous. Because of that, it was almost as if the people around me didn't exist. There would be no consequences; my actions would leave no imprint. Even if someone insulted me, I wouldn't know enough French slang to understand what they said.

So, without any internal debate, I confidently pulled my arms out of the straps of my one-piece (did you really imagine I owned a bikini?), pulled my tank suit down, and like a half-peeled banana, into the water I went. Quickly.

There I was, topless in the Mediterranean, the tops of my breasts gleaming white like the top halves of two hard-boiled eggs. I felt empowered and alive and silky and sensuous. I felt like a woman capable of enticing an attractive French man, spending the evening with him, and then making out at dawn (in a public place) before we caught separate trains — without ever learning his last name. For the first time in my life, I was in total possession of my femininity. Electric. Powerful. Élan-y. I was a brand new, sexy, anonymous me.

Then, from just off to the side of me, I heard:

"You go to Unnamed East Coast University, don't you?"

As it so happens, I did.

I turned to see a serious-looking guy, my age, standing in the water right next to me. He was one of those people who, no matter what he was actually wearing, always wore wide wale corduroy pants in his mind.

"We've met before. I'm Brad Lastname's roommate."

Brad Lastname was a friend at school. He had a brief, unrequited crush on me before graduating, winning a great deal of money in the lottery, marrying the man of his dreams, and posting extensively on Facebook. And here Brad's roommate happened to be, on that particular day in Europe, in the South of France, in Cannes, no less, in the Mediterranean Sea. I lowered myself, feeling the water flirt with my chin.

What are the odds?

"Oh yeah, hi."

"So, you are studying abroad?"

"Yup."

It was a typical, banal conversation except for the fact that under the water, my breasts were running free and we both knew it. That knowledge was the only thing that could have possibly given our conversation a sexual charge.

"You have a Eurail pass?"

"I do."

"The two-month one?"

"No, the one month. You can't use it in England. That's the BritRail pass."

Needless to say, we did not make out. When he left, I pulled up my suit, put the straps back on, and left the water. And quite honestly, my mind is a blank after that. I have no recollection of anything else. It was all I could do to get away. Nature, or a higher power had sent me a crystal-clear message.

Stop trying to be fabulous.

Was there any other conclusion I could draw? The lesson was laid out before me, Nathaniel Hawthorne-style. I was Hester Prynne, only there was no place to sew my "A."

I'd like to say that experience helped me discover the self-love and acceptance I needed to express my own uniqueness and to use the word "fabulous" about myself without a hint of sarcasm. But I can't.

As I've gotten older though, I've learned a few things. Maybe you already know them, but humor me.

First off, it's not what women wear, or do, that makes them fabulous. It's not about joining or following or copying anyone else. Women are fabulous when they dare to express their true selves — from the inside out, unapologetically for all to see, with no need for positive affirmation. They're fabulous when they carry themselves with a confidence and boldness that no roommate of Brad Lastname could ever shake. That courage is what we all find so compelling.

And they're fabulous when they do it in their home countries.

Secondly, I have grown to understand that you rarely remember the days when nothing goes wrong. They have little traction in your memory. Moments like my Cannes experience are pearls, strung on the same thread with the day I was the only kid at Hebrew school that dressed up for Purim (as Queen Esther), and the time my cousins and I entertained my date by dancing to "Sledgehammer." It's a necklace I don't wear every day, but it comes in handy at parties.

And finally, age has allowed me to appreciate that I am not the norm. I laugh loudly and insanely enough to make heads turn in annoyance. I make instant pudding with half the milk required, because I like the mortar-like consistency. My hand gestures don't illuminate what I say. And I get way too way too much joy from the $1 IKEA breakfast to be truly mainstream.

I am authentic. Isn't that fabulous?

Jenna is a writer and an alum of Second City in Chicago, where she wrote and performed shows alongside Stephen Colbert, Tina Fey and others. She has been on the writing staff of such shows as MADtv *and Steve Martin's* The Downer Channel *as well as a guest writer on* Saturday Night Live.

Authenticity is fabulous. How are you "not the norm?" List five quirks and idiosyncrasies that you have grown to appreciate about yourself.

"Remember no one can make you feel inferior without your consent."

~ Eleanor Roosevelt

A Shy TV Anchor

I am a shy person at my core, but no one believes this because for almost 40 years, I made my living as a TV news anchor and reporter.

It's true, though. When I was little, I was so shy that I wouldn't go trick-or-treating. My brothers and sisters would come back with huge bags of candy, dumping them on the floor and running out again for more. I can still see them, breathless with sugar-charged excitement, trying to get me to come along, but the idea of knocking on the doors of *strangers* or even neighbors was just too terrifying.

Having to sell Girl Scout cookies door-to-door was torture. At one home, the lady made my sister and me come inside to *kvell* over our little uniforms. I wore one of those little Brownie beanies. I still remember the *kvelling* — INSIDE A STRANGER'S HOUSE. It was mortifying.

What I enjoyed most was playing by myself in our small backyard. My dad made me a bird feeder, and in the spring the birds would nest in the hawthorn trees next to my bedroom window. My favorite childhood memory is watching the whole nesting process, from the egg-laying all the way to that amazing day when the chicks fledged on unsteady wing, with their nervous parents shrieking hysterically.

I was a living stereotype of the nice little Japanese girl: quiet, polite, and obedient. My mom worried that I would spend my life being stepped on like a doormat. She told me she spent much of her own life as a doormat, and the idea of me repeating that experience saddened her. My poor mom raised five kids, pretty much on her own. One of my brothers is disabled and one sister had emotional problems, and my dad could never really handle it. If one of us did something wrong (and you know how kids are), he would go nuts, yelling, and often hitting my brothers.

This had a huge effect on all of us. I learned not to do anything wrong. I learned how to avoid conflict.

Staying under the radar was something the whole Japanese American community did. The WWII Internment Camps had only closed in 1946, and our parents were busy trying to reestablish their homes and businesses. We lived with this unspoken truth: *you could lose everything in a moment because of your race.* There was less chance of that if we avoided conflict and studied hard. We set out to prove that we were good Americans.

All of this made me even less willing to take gambles and just reinforced my need to seek approval. Add being shy to that mix and you get the picture.

At some point, though, I began to see that being shy, quiet, and obedient meant you rarely got what you wanted. Sometimes you didn't even KNOW what you wanted because you were so used to being obedient.

My disabled brother and sister NEVER got what they wanted. Neither did my mom.

All these quiet realizations led to **THE MOMENT.** I don't personally remember this moment, but my mom did, and she recounted **THE MOMENT** in vivid terms:

I was about 10 years old, and quietly (as usual) sitting at the kitchen table with my mom and her friend. My mom was talking about how worried she was about my siblings, when suddenly, as she tells it, I hit my fist on the table and announced, "I'm not going to be like that!!"

She was stunned. Such a dramatic pronouncement from her shy, obedient child was totally out of character.

But in fact, after **THE MOMENT**, I began to change.

I don't remember thinking any of this through at the time, nor was I consciously aware of how badly I wanted something different for myself. What I do remember is slowly starting my own little assertiveness training program, forcing myself to be more *out there*. Looking back, this took some serious willpower. I ramped up those efforts when we moved to a new neighborhood and I had to meet new kids.

It was hard at first, foisting myself on strangers. I had to force myself to say "hi" and to start a conversation. It felt almost out-of-body strange — like acting — very inorganic.

One day, I found an old copy of *How to Make Friends and Influence People* among my dad's old books. That book taught me a lot. It taught me to break the ice by asking questions. I learned to listen well, and I came to realize that I was actually pretty good at making other people feel comfortable. I think this process helped me recognize that, even though I was shy, I had natural communication skills.

High school for me became all about making friends and influencing people. Our school had a large percentage of Asian students — in fact our entire top 10 were Asian. But the Asian children of tiger moms were not getting what they wanted — they were keeping their heads down and worrying about grades. I really did not want to be stuck in that box. I became loud, opinionated, and outgoing. I was a cheerleader.

During college, Asian Americans were joining the larger civil rights movement. Being Japanese American became something I felt proud of, instead of something I felt I had to overcome. Women were pushing for equal rights — no more doormats. I was getting outside reinforcement to break stereotypes and to reach for something larger. I changed my major from Elementary Education to Political Science.

By the time I finished college and started thinking about a career, I was a more complex person — still shy inside, but with a learned ability to push past that, and meet, greet, and pursue.

A Japanese American woman had just started reporting on local TV in Seattle. This was historic in the '70s, because women and African Americans were just starting to break into news, but no other people of color. Barbara Tanabe was the first Asian American. When she came on, my father would yell, "BARBARA'S ON TV!" and we'd all come running into the living room to watch.

Maybe I could do that, I thought . . . This thought would never have occurred to me without seeing Barbara on TV.

Someone knew Barbara and arranged for me to shadow her in the newsroom one morning. At some point during that visit, I recognized deep in my gut, this was where I belonged. This was what I really wanted.

Shyness can end your career in a newsroom. But the best thing I had going for me, shy or not, was persistence. That was crucial in landing that first on-air job, and later, in getting information. If someone said no, I had to find a way around it.

When I got my first job as a reporter, we had to have our scripts checked by the Managing Editor. I would stand politely in line while other reporters simply jumped in front of me. "Sorry Tokuda, I'm on deadline," or "I'm late. I need to get in here!" I would think to myself in my small, shy voice, "I'm on a deadline too . . ."

I had to learn to push my way in, stand my ground, and stop letting people jump in front of me. I forced myself way out of my comfort zone to approach strangers and get "man-on-the-street" interviews. Again, it felt awkward and inorganic at first, but I pushed through that feeling and just did it.

Having a microphone and a photographer at my side gave me a power I'd never had. "Excuse me, Channel 5 here," I learned to say, walking taller. The waters would part, and we'd move through the crowd.

Another thing I liked about reporting — we weren't IN the conflict; we were COVERING it. We were trained to be fair. Not to take sides, but to find the truth. The truth would speak for itself.

Reporting involved skills that regularly pushed me out of my cocoon — asking a lot of questions was the only way to get a story, and speaking out was the only way to be heard. I found that I had a competitive, ambitious side too, which seemed to grow with success.

One day my mother asked me, "Which are you? The shy little girl or the pushy broad?" I thought about it, and answered, "I guess I'm both."

The truth was, sometimes, that pushy bravado still felt a little forced. It would take many years for me to find the boundaries of what I was really made of and to feel truly integrated, whole, and authentic. It took successes and failures and *life* to develop true confidence.

I was in my 50s by then . . .

I'm retired now. As I've gotten older, I care less about what others think, but the shy thing never totally goes away.

I still feel shy when we go to parties with a lot of strangers or if I meet an important person. During a recent election, I had to gather all my courage to hand out leaflets at the farmer's market for a friend who was running for office. For the most part, I now accept shyness as one of the many characteristics that make me who I am.

By the way, I have several bird feeders now. I am back out in the garden and spend hours in the forest doing environmental restoration work. It's very healing after all those years of pushing. I am enjoying a quiet peace.

Wendy Tokuda was a San Francisco Bay Area television staple for more than 30 years, as both TV news anchor and feature reporter. She retired from broadcast journalism in 2016.

When do you tend to be shy? When do you tend to be "pushy?" When do you feel like you have to overcompensate for a natural tendency of your own?

"Can't nobody fly with all that shit. Wanna fly, you got to give up the shit that weighs you down."

~ Toni Morrison

ELISABETH SHARP MCKETTA

Moist: A Journey Out of Chapstick Addiction

When my daughter was born, we had to go straight to the Neonatal Intensive Care Unit, because breathing was harder for her than it should've been. They put an IV in her hand, and when it wore out after a day, they put it in her other hand. Then, in her foot. Then, in her other foot. I watched each part of her 7-pound 10-ounce body turn scaly as it got wrapped with IV tape and parched by the dry air of the NICU. I wanted to rub oil onto her extremities. I wanted to touch each dry part and make it moist, but she was connected to wires and away from home, not ready for me yet.

Every part of her dried out that first week of her life: her eyes, her small inverted nipples, her fingers. Everything but her lips. Her lips stayed perfect — soft and moist.

I talked to her even when I couldn't hold her. I told her about myself, about the things I had learned. I told her, one evening, about need. About how important it is to need people, and not things. How not needing too many things makes a person portable, able to travel light. I told her things I learned almost a decade ago, from being addicted to lip balm.

Since discovering lip balm at age ten, I put it on my lips between fifty to a hundred times a day. These are real numbers, by the way, not fuzzy math. I had to keep it with me at all times: I had vanilla lip balm in my glove compartment; Nivea rose in the pocket of whichever boyfriend I was dating; standard cherry in my backpack; Body Shop strawberry next to my bed; Rachel Perry banana-coconut in the kitchen; and my favorite of all, Montana huckleberry in my purse — that one I always ordered in bulk in case I ran out.

Jump forward eleven years — I had just graduated from college, and I used the first paycheck of my first writing job to book a trip to New York. I packed clothes for a week, my notebook, a toothbrush, and half a dozen tubes of lip balm: plain mint, gooey grape in a tub, Dr. Pepper-flavored, banana-coconut, lemon-lime, Montana huckleberry.

I stayed with my friend Helena who was a first-year medical student, and spent my first day exploring. When Helena finished class, I met her for oysters at a little restaurant near Battery Park. I was telling her about my day when she interrupted me and said: "Hey, Liz, when's the last time you looked in the mirror?"

"What?" I asked. "I don't know. This morning, probably. Why?"

"Well," she said, "I was just wondering what's wrong with your lips."

She ushered me off to the bathroom to have a look.

Both my top and bottom lips looked as if they had been burned. They had this awful blistery flakiness, and had turned a bright lipstick burgundy. The corners of my mouth had cracked into sore-looking circles, sort of like the red dots on clown-cheeks.

Perhaps, I thought, I needed better lip balm. I dragged Helena out of the oyster bar and to a Walgreen's a few doors down. I bought a new tube of Vaseline lip therapy and thought that by the end of the night, the problem would be solved.

But the next morning, my lips had gotten worse. When I got up for breakfast, Helena was sitting at her kitchen table, practicing her sutures on a piece of raw chicken, and still she looked at my mouth and said, "Gross."

In addition, she began trying to diagnose me, telling me all the things it "might" be, such as oral cancer. "That's what it looks like," she said apologetically. "Oh, I hope it's not squamous cell carcinoma! Or worse . . . what if it's syphilis? If it is syphilis, you'd better treat it — untreated syphilis can lead to blindness. Or you might have Steven-Johnson Syndrome. That wouldn't be too bad — except that it's untreatable."

I still thought the problem was as simple as my needing more lip balm, so I went out and bought something stronger, with soothing herbs and lavender.

But this new lip balm didn't work either, and my face was getting worse; the cakey redness was spreading down toward my chin and up toward my nose. So, I cut my trip short and went home that day. As I took the subway back to my apartment, I noticed tactless people — mostly children — staring at me. It was disconcerting.

That evening, I had had enough. I had two more weeks before my college health insurance ran out, so I gathered every lip balm I owned and frog-marched myself to University Health Services. I wasn't sure which floor to go to — was this an Ear, Nose, and Throat Problem, or simply Dermatology? Should I go to Sexual Health, or the Cancer Center? It turned out that all the different wings closed at 5pm, so any problems afterward were considered Emergency.

So I waited in the University Health Campus Emergency Center, sitting among people with broken limbs, debilitating coughs, and mysterious silent ailments that did not betray themselves. I waited a long time.

Finally, I got called back. The doctor looked exhausted, like those interns you see in movies who haven't slept for the better part of a week. "Well?" he said. "What is the problem?"

I explained about my mouth.

"Did you try lip balm?" he asked.

"Yes!" I said. "About twenty different kinds!" And I opened my purse, and out spilled plain mint, gooey grape in a tub, Dr. Pepper-flavored, banana-coconut, lemon-lime, Montana huckleberry, and dozens of other kinds that I had tried and that had failed me.

The doctor wanted to know how long I had been using lip balm. I told him eleven years.

Then he asked: "How many times a day would you say you use it?"

I decided to give a conservative answer. "About thirty," I said, casually. "Give or take."

"Thirty!" He said, "Jesus." It dawned on me then that this had to be serious, as the doctor probably wasn't supposed to say "Jesus" in front of patients.

He put on gloves and examined my mouth. He took a culture. He left the room and returned a few minutes later, and said: "The problem is that you are addicted to lip balm." He went on to say that my lips had stopped producing moisture, and that the only way to fix this was for me to go cold turkey.

I told him that wasn't an option. I asked, "Can't you send me home with, like, a prescription or something? What is normally done in these cases?"

He gave me a scornful look. "We don't see a lot of lip balm addicts in the emergency room."

But he disappeared again and returned with a sample tube of steroid cream, the kind you use for athlete's foot. "You may put the cream on your lips twice a day. No more. If you come back here in a week addicted to this cream, I will refuse to see you." Then he left the room for good, leaving me in it, surrounded with colored lip balm tubes poking in all different directions.

It was a sad walk home that Saturday night, but I stopped at a trashcan in Harvard Square, surrounded by punky teenagers and homeless people, and I summoned the courage to empty my purse. Down went plain mint, gooey grape in a tub; down went Dr. Pepper-flavored, banana-coconut, lemon-lime. Down went all tubes, including Montana huckleberry.

There is an invisible line dividing before and after in most addictions, and even in such a ridiculous one, the line existed.

The things I couldn't do until my lips healed included kissing (when I tried to kiss my boyfriend, he refused because he said I was "scaly"); eating spicy food; taking big bites of any food; and using lipstick. I learned this last rule a month after the initial flare-up, when I tried to test the doctor's orders by using moisturizing lipstick — and I ended up, once again, with starchy clown-lips that took another month to heal.

But soon I learned that there were also things I could now do: for example, swimming. I used to have to stick near the sides of the pool or the lake, because even in the water I needed to have fast access to lip balm. But now when I went swimming with friends, I could swim out further. I could also travel more lightly, since I no longer needed to carry a purse to tote around all my lip balms. I could just stick money and keys in my pocket and go.

And it made me wonder: what other things did I think I needed that I could give up?

First on that list was the boyfriend. He was a place-holder — good company but certainly not the love of my life — also, I could not get him to stop using the word "irregardless," which is not actually a word.

I thought: I don't need him.

Then I realized how many belongings I had that I didn't need. That year after college, I started giving them away. It was sort of the beginning of my life as a generous person. If I wasn't using something well, I felt that the thing should go to somebody who would love it.

I moved into a smaller apartment. I looked at my life and all its commitments — did I truly need to be a member of this club? Was that friend actually a good friend? Did I need this job, or was I just wasting my time and keeping it to feel safe? I reexamined every thing, every person, and every commitment that I had. And I consciously chose to either keep them or let them go. I began traveling lightly in a whole new way, choosing to focus my time and energy only on the things that mattered to me.

And that's how lip balm became a divider between my teens and my twenties, an addiction that I left behind in one decade to move, unaddicted, into the next.

Elisabeth Sharp McKetta is the author of She Never Told Me about the Ocean *and eight previous books. "Moist" also appears in her first essay collection,* Awake with Asashoryu, *published by Paul Dry Books in 2022. Elisabeth teaches writing for Harvard and Oxford, and she lives with her sea-swimmer husband and two young children.*

Stopping one bad habit can initiate the domino effect of looking at other things that don't serve you well or that you don't "need." What have you stopped or walked away from to lighten your own load?

"Life shrinks or expands
in proportion to one's courage."

~ Anaïs Nin

MELISSA HAYNES

A Lifelong Dream Realized

Dreamers spend their lives asleep.
  The early bird gets the worm.
  Keep your head down and work hard.
  Your job is your worth.
  Without a job, you are worthless.
  If you don't have a good job, you don't have anything.
  Money makes the world go round.
  You are your bank balance.
  Your title defines you.
  Appearance is everything.
  Grow up.
  Get real.
My father, at the head of the dining room table every Sunday night, preached the same speech. His words were easier to digest than the overcooked roast beef and soggy vegetables my mother was proud of.

His well-meaning words born out of his fear were meant to instill a strong work ethic, but as a five-year-old, I adopted these words as my own, as any child would. They grew with me into my own beliefs, identity, and values.

In *The Impersonal Life*, author Joseph Benner says beliefs are merely the "rubbish you have gathered from the dumping grounds of others."

This is a story of rubbish removal told from the best viewpoint possible: hindsight.

It was 2010. I had spent the last three decades desperately trying to fulfill my so-called identity, born from my father's fears. It started with selling chocolates door-to-door at six, then a paper route at age eight, and led me to where I was now — about to finish the 2010 Olympics and with it my job as an Olympic project manager. Recession would follow the Games; the economy was already contracting and the torch hadn't even left town yet.

Thousands would be looking for jobs and they told us to prepare to be unemployed for at least a year — perhaps two. The prospect of being jobless, aka worthless, for two years was unfathomable. Lucky for me, I didn't have to be. I had an offer to sit at the head of a company in an industry I knew inside-and-out. The Head of an established company. The Boss. The Big Cheese. The 'Shit.' I had finally fulfilled my purpose — to be worthy.

My father would finally be proud, if he were still alive.

The job wouldn't be easy; I'd work long hours at least six days a week, and not have much of a life outside of work; something that was strangely alluring in the past. So why then, was I hesitating to take it?

It was *the nudge*. The nudge is the whisper of the Soul.

Mine was saying, "Turn down the job."

Have you heard the nudge within you? Is yours a whisper or a scream?

While I stood at the crossroads of what perhaps was the biggest (in hindsight) decision of my life, the nudge was too powerful to ignore.

Would I dare to fail? Would I dare to be embarrassed when I fell flat on my face? Would I dare to be judged? Would I dare to let my bullshit identity die? Would I dare to expunge the one thing that defined me: my job? Would I dare to challenge my lifelong beliefs?

The temptation of comfort and the known was great, but the possibility of living a muted life was even greater.

I turned down the job and dared to do what the five-year-old me used to daydream about while buried in the pages of *National*

Geographic magazines in my kindergarten reading corner (before the rubbish beliefs had muted that dream.)

I would go to Africa to volunteer with big African animals (little did I know, it was they who would end up saving me).

At the time, I wasn't sure if I had just made the best or worst decision of my life. I was leaning towards the latter. But now, from the vantage point of the hind, I can see it was the best damn decision I ever made.

After researching many organizations and projects, I decided on a Big Five conservation project, volunteering with an organization called Edge of Africa. I liked that the project was small and hands-on.

Three months later, I arrived in a tiny pocket of South Africa, just off the Garden Route to a small game reserve. The reserve was home to rescues of the Big Five: lions who had been saved from a trophy-hunting farm, elephants whose herds were annihilated by poachers and sent to be touring elephants — a fate they rebelled against so they ended up here. Rhinoceros, giraffes, wildebeest, buffalo, crocodiles, plus many other animals also called this place home.

I arrived and met my boss, a khaki-clad, burly ranger ten years my junior named Gary. He took one look at me and said, "Let me guess. You're here because you dreamed of Africa."

"Yes! My whole life!" I exclaimed.

"Mmm. Well, you better wake up, Canada, otherwise that dream is going to become a nightmare. This is a working game reserve. These are wild animals."

"Okay."

"You'll be sleeping alone over there in that tent. That electrical wire mostly keeps the animals out."

"Okay." I said, with hesitation.

My tent camp was a small triangular plot on the edge of the reserve. Nothing but a thin electrical wire, serving merely as a 'mental block' to the animals, was all that separated me from them.

The lion camp bordered one side. The elephant camp was on the other side and the open reserve was on the last. The lions were so close that I could hear their roars every night. Needless to say, I didn't sleep a wink that first night — or maybe it was many nights . . .

Work began at dawn and ended at dinnertime. The first time I put on the soft, butter-yellow work gloves, I never felt prouder. That is, until I began to actually work. Have you ever lifted elephant dung? That shit's heavy!

Mucking out elephant stalls took hours of backbreaking, stinky work. But you know what? I loved every grueling second of it.

Days were spent patrolling the reserve, tending to the animals, tracking cheetahs, and doing overall reserve maintenance. Working with the animals was exhilarating. Every day I gave of myself, trying desperately to even out the balance sheet, but the more I gave, the more I received — forever indebted to the animals of Africa and to the ranger's great patience!

A few days in, the worst storm of over a century pummeled the game reserve. Our conservation effort quickly morphed into a massive clean-up effort. Rebuilding roads by hand, one stone at a time. Chopping reeds from within a crocodile pit to relieve the flooding. Cutting tree branches. Our only tool for all these jobs — a machete.

One of the casualties from the storm was a red hartebeest, a regal creature. She didn't die instantly; it would take a few days. It was heartbreaking, but she showed me the perfection of nature and life in her passing, as they call it in Africa: the circle of life.

Her remains would feed other animals; something is always passed on in death to the living, in both the wild world and ours. It was a gift that would release me from my grief over my mother's passing a few years before.

Soon, I no longer feared sleeping in my tent; the lull of the roar of the lions put me to sleep every night. In fact, I feared nothing and was ready to confront a lifelong phobia: Great White Sharks.

I believed, thanks to the 1975 blockbuster *Jaws*, that Great White Sharks were man-eating predators.

Three weeks later. Mossel Bay, South Africa. Pumped-up from my experience thus far, I shivered with fear as I climbed into the titanium shark cage. There we waited in the deep blue darkness and silence, save for the loud thumping of my heart.

And then it began.

The cage began to rock. Not from the current, but from the massive weight of the creature that had just passed behind us. I tried to look, but only caught a glimpse of a dark shadow disappearing into the blue. The terror was overwhelming. What was I thinking, doing this???

I reminded myself to breathe.

Within minutes, shark after shark came to check us out, one even pushing his nose through the cage just inches in front of my face. Oh my God! Would he bite my head off? Smash the cage? No. He would retreat and move on just as quickly as he had arrived.

My hand was on the outside of the cage and a 20-foot female jetted in front of it.

Contact.

Shivers.

Reverence.

My lifelong phobia was nothing more than a Hollywood-induced illusion.

My fear instantly morphed into profound love for this misrepresented creature; a graceful, inquisitive, powerful predator who keeps the oceans in balance and now, after surviving millions of years, is endangered by the hand of the greatest super predator of all: humans.

As the sea turned pink with sunset, my old beliefs sunk as fast as the sun.

I was becoming me for the first time.

Every one of us has the nudge inside, nudging us towards that which will ignite our Soul.

When we have the courage to listen and act on the nudge, we begin to experience an adventure that is ours, rewriting our beliefs and values with our own pen as we discover who we really are — without the rubbish.

Melissa Haynes is a shark advocate, animal lover, adventure junkie, conservationist, and author of the book, Learning to Play with a Lion's Testicles.

A prompt from Melissa:

The nudge is quiet, to hear it you must go within, in silence.

Do you remember your daydreams when you still believed they were possible?

Do you have any beliefs keeping you from hearing your nudge?

How could you rewrite those beliefs to honor your experience?

What courageous actions can you take now?

"Smile in the mirror.
Do that every morning, and you'll
start to see a big difference in your life."

~ Yoko Ono

REBECCA CHAMAA

Revealing My Secret:
I Have Paranoid Schizophrenia

I am a simple woman. Most mornings, I get up; make coffee; write my blog; make a spinach, banana, yogurt, and berry smoothie; take my medication; and check-in with my social media accounts. My husband says I am easy to please. He gets the coffee ready some mornings before I wake up, and I feel like it's my birthday. There is joy in my heart about routine and all the little things.

I have paranoid schizophrenia, and I know how bad a day can be. I can have social anxiety, general anxiety, or paranoid thoughts that leave me fearful. On the worst days of my life, I have been psychotic, a condition of the mind I wish no one had to experience.

For most of my adult life, I have lived in a bubble along with my husband. We have protected ourselves and kept our lives very private, even from close friends, in order to avoid judgment, ridicule, jokes, and special treatment.

When I say special treatment, I mean people behaving toward us in specific ways not based on our personalities, accomplishments, or behavior, but on assumptions surrounding my diagnosis. Recently, we decided to pop that bubble in a massive and public way.

My husband and I posted an article on Facebook that one of my mentors wrote about my courage. The courage she was referring to was my honesty in my writing groups about an illness I have battled since my 20s: the illness of schizophrenia. My writing groups were the only place where everyone was aware of my diagnosis. I simply couldn't write poetry and memoir without revealing details of my mental illness, because much of my writing has to do with situations related to having and struggling with schizophrenia.

Before my husband and I went public with the secret we kept for over 17 years, we had many discussions about how people might react and how we'd respond. We had some near-sleepless nights and felt very anxious, sensing that our entire world was about to change.

In response to our posting, we received emails, calls, texts, Facebook messages, and letters in the mail. Most people have been very supportive, at least on the surface. I say that not to diminish their support, but to be honest. There is so much misinformation about schizophrenia (like, that it's multiple personality disorder, dissociative identity disorder, or that people with schizophrenia wear tinfoil hats or do other bizarre things) that people respond from ignorance rather than understanding.

You can indeed see some people with schizophrenia living on the street, talking to voices only they can hear. It is also true that some people with schizophrenia are in jails instead of hospitals. But these scenarios point to a broken system and not to everyone who has schizophrenia. The people I know with schizophrenia are trying to live as normally as possible while struggling with a brain disease.

Unfortunately, mental illness is more common than most people know or admit. The National Alliance for the Mentally Ill (NAMI) reports that one in five Americans will develop a mental illness in their lifetime. Those numbers suggest that everyone reading this knows at least one person (probably more) who has battled with, or is currently battling with, a mental illness.

We have come a long way in accepting depression. And because of some very high-profile people, we have come a long way in accepting bipolar disorder. Still, we have not moved forward much regarding the stigma surrounding schizophrenia. Schizophrenia is still wildly misunderstood, and the people who suffer from it (openly) are often left out, or pushed out of everyday social situations.

Daily, I am subjected to people making jokes about hearing voices or paranoid delusions that people with a mental illness might experience. Of course, the words "psycho," "nuts," "crazy," "schitzo," "whacked," "mental," "loony," etc., are all part of our everyday vocabulary.

I stayed in that bubble for almost 20 years because I feared that the world would judge me. I was afraid that everything I said and did would be considered a symptom of my illness rather than part of my personality or character. And to be honest, in the case of many people, some of my worst fears have come true.

But even with that, I'm not sorry that we popped the bubble. I am now free to be me, both in public and in private, and I have the chance to use my life and my experience to help fight the stigma that left me in hiding all those years.

Maybe my honesty will make it easier for the next person to share. Hopefully, I can and will be a voice that helps pave a new path for those who want to live out in the open.

I don't wish for a bigger house, a fancier car, designer clothes, or the latest in plastic surgery. I am happy with what I have. I am thankful for a day without voices keeping me from communicating with my husband or friends. I am grateful for a day without the terror that I have died and gone to hell and there is no way out. I am thankful for a day that I don't believe I am being poisoned or tape-recorded or followed. I am grateful for a day I don't think God has chosen me to be a prophet or healer.

The medication I take keeps me from experiencing psychosis, but I still experience symptoms of my illness every day. You wouldn't know it to look at me, but I have a great deal of paranoia around food and eating issues. I spend ninety percent of my time alone because I become easily overwhelmed in social settings. I have a group of good friends, and I love spending time with them, but I lack social motivation. Any kind of motivation is a struggle.

It's okay, though. I have a good life. I have a roof over my head, running water, a comfortable bed, and access to laundry facilities, transportation, and good medical care. I am never really hungry or thirsty. I have someone who loves and cares about me. I am not living with war or famine. The condition of my life is so much better than billions of people on the planet. I won't complain.

Sure, living with paranoid schizophrenia is difficult, but millions of other things are, as well. Cancer is difficult. Diabetes is difficult. Parkinson's and Alzheimer's are difficult. Who is to say which challenge is more complex? Who is to say who has the more difficult path to walk? We walk in the direction we have to, and, in my case, I look for the good along the way.

There is so much good, like a pink sunset, the laughter of a child, an unexpected call from a friend, french fries with lemon juice, and feta cheese.

Mine is a beautiful life, even if some people wouldn't agree. Too much negativity is a disability, but it is not the disability I have.

Rebecca Chamaa's work has been published in Glamour, Good Housekeeping, Teen Vogue, Business Insider, Hope for Women, Woman Alive, *and other magazines. She also wrote a book titled,* Pills, Poetry & Prose: Life with Schizophrenia.

A prompt from Rebecca: Write about a struggle you have, or write about something people don't know about you.

"The most courageous act is still to think for yourself. Aloud."

~ Coco Chanel

On Self-Esteem

As wise women and men in every culture tell us: The art of life is not controlling what happens to us, but using what happens to us.

Like all great oaks, this understanding began with a very small acorn.

It was the late sixties, those days that were still pre-feminist for me. I didn't question the fact that male journalists with less experience than I were getting the political assignments that were my real interest. Instead, I was grateful to be writing profiles of visiting celebrities — a departure from the fashion and family subjects that female reporters were usually given — and this included an interview that was to take place over tea in the Palm Court of the Plaza Hotel.

Because the actor was very late, I waited while the assistant manager circled disapprovingly and finally approached. "Unescorted ladies," he announced loudly, were "absolutely not allowed" in the lobby. I told him I was a reporter waiting for an arriving guest who couldn't be contacted any other way — an explanation that sounded lame even to me. The manager escorted me firmly past curious bystanders and out the lobby door. I was humiliated. Did I look like a prostitute? Was my trench coat too battered — or not battered enough? I was anxious: How was I going to find my subject and do my work? I decided to wait outside the revolving door in the hope of spotting the famous actor through its glass, but an hour passed with no success.

Later, I learned that he had arrived, failed to see me, and left. His press agent called my editor to complain that I had "stood up" his client. The actor missed his publicity, the editor missed a deadline, and I missed a check that I needed to pay the rent. I also blamed myself for not figuring out how to "get the story" and worried about being demoted permanently back to the ghetto of "women's interest" articles I was trying to escape.

By coincidence a month or so later, I was assigned to interview another celebrity who was also staying at the Plaza. To avoid a similar fiasco, I had arranged to meet this one in his suite, but on my way through the lobby, I noticed my former nemesis standing guard. Somehow, I found myself lingering, as if rooted to the spot — and sure enough, the manager approached me with his same officious speech. But this time I was amazed to hear myself saying some very different things. I told him this was a public place where I had every legal right to be, and asked why he hadn't banished the several "unescorted men" in the lobby who might be male prostitutes. I also pointed out that since hotel staffs were well known to supply call girls in return for a percentage of their pay, perhaps he was just worried about losing a commission.

He looked quite startled — and let me stay. I called my subject and suggested we have tea downstairs after all. It turned out to be a newsworthy interview, and I remember writing it up with more ease than usual and delivering it with an odd sense of well-being.

What was the lesson of these two incidents? Clearly, the assistant manager and I were unchanged. I was even wearing the same trench coat and freelancing for the same publication. Only one thing was different: my self-esteem. It had been raised almost against my will — by contagion.

Between those two interviews, a woman doctor had made a reservation for herself and a party of friends at the Plaza's Oak Room, a public restaurant that was maintained as a male-only bastion at lunchtime on the grounds that female voices might disturb men's business meetings. When this woman was stopped at the Oak Room door for being the wrong gender of "Dr.," as she knew she would be, her lunch group of distinguished feminists turned into a spirited sidewalk picket line and held a press conference they had called in advance.

Now, I had also been invited to join this protest — and refused. In New York as in most cities, there were many public restaurants and bars that either excluded women altogether or wouldn't serve "unescorted ladies" (that is, any woman or group of women without the magical presence of one man). Certainly, I resented this, but protesting it in the Oak Room, a restaurant too expensive for most people, male or female, seemed a mistake. The only remedy was a city council ordinance banning discrimination in public places, and that would require democratic support. Besides, feminists were already being misrepresented in the media as white, middle class, and frivolous, a caricature that even then I knew was wrong: the first feminists I had heard of in the sixties were working-class women who broke the sex barrier in factory assembly lines, and the first I actually met were black women on welfare who compared that demeaning system to a gigantic husband who demanded sexual faithfulness (the no-man-in-the- house rule) in return for subsistence payments. If groups like those were not publicized — and if well-to-do women who lunched at the Plaza were — I feared this new movement's image would become even more distorted.

As it turned out, I was right about tactics and the media's continuing image of feminism: "whitemiddleclass" did become like one key o the typewriter of many journalists (though polls showed that black women were almost twice as likely to support feminist changes than white women were). But I was very wrong about women' responses — including my own. For instance: By the time of that demonstration at the Plaza, I already had picketed for civil rights, against U.S. involvement in Vietnam, and with migrant farm workers, often in demonstrations that were far from tactically perfect; so why was I suddenly demanding perfection of women? When blacks or Jews had been kept out of restaurants and bars, expensive or not, I felt fine about protesting; so why couldn't I take my own half of the human race (which, after all, included half of all blacks and half of all Jews) just as seriously?

The truth was that I had internalized society's unserious estimate of all that was female — including myself. This was low self-esteem, not logic. Should a black woman demonstrate for the right to eat at dime-store lunch counters in the South, where she was barred by race, and then quietly leave when refused service at an expensive New York restaurant on account of sex? Of course not. The principle — and, more important, the result for one real woman — was the same. But I had been raised to consider any judgment based on sex alone less important than any judgment based on race, class, or anything else alone. In fact, if you counted up all the groups in the world other than white women, I was valuing just about everybody more than I valued myself.

Nonetheless, all the excuses of my conscious mind couldn't keep my unconscious self from catching the contagious spirit of those women who picketed the Oak Room. When I faced the hotel manager again, I had glimpsed the world as if women mattered. By seeing through their eyes, I had begun to see through my own.

Gloria Steinem is a writer and activist who has been involved in feminist and other social justice issues for over forty years. A major figure in the launch of the women's movement in the 1960s, she is one of the few to span generations and cultures with such newer U.S. feminist groups as the 3rd Wave and Choice USA, as well as international human rights/ women's rights groups including Equality Now. Steinem is the co-founder of New York Magazine *and* Ms. Magazine, *and author of such touchstone books as* Outrageous Acts and Everyday Rebellions; Revolution from Within, *and* Moving Beyond Words, *among other influential writing.*

What cultural norms or societal rules have caused you to internalize or accept a lower sense of self-worth? How have you defied those norms, spoken up, or become active in an effort to change them?

"Your opponent, in the end, is never really
the player on the other side of the net,
or the swimmer in the next lane,
or the team on the other side of the field,
or even the bar you must high-jump.
Your opponent is yourself,
your negative internal voices,
your level of determination."

~ Grace Lichtenstein

PIPPY LONGSTALKER

Roller Derby: The New Self-Help Sport

Let me introduce myself. My name is Pippy Longstalker. I'm a long-time roller derby skater, and my number is 36. I began skating with the Dominion Derby Girls in 2009, and I have loved every minute of it. Roller derby is a full-contact sport that requires agility, skill, teamwork, and most of all, confidence in yourself.

The Dominion Derby Girls is an all-female flat track roller derby league formed with the purpose of promoting the sport of roller derby and giving back to the community. The Women's Flat Track Derby Association governs their rules and regulations, but there are other governing bodies, rules, and types of tracks, such as banked track. Above all, roller derby leagues and teams are amateur athletic organizations, priding themselves on the diversity and inclusivity of their members. Skaters, officials, and other members have rigorous training and practice schedules that enable them to take part in local, national, and even international competitions.

My interest in roller derby began in 2005 and happened by proxy through my sister, who skated with the Rose City Rollers in Portland, Oregon. She was looking for an athletic-, social-, and community-oriented organization, and that's when she started learning how to skate.

She skated competitively for many years and is still very close friends with some of her old teammates. While I enjoyed watching her compete, life took me on a different path with various moves across the country.

I eventually moved to Virginia, 3,000 miles away from my sister and my family. I love exercise, so I was running on a treadmill and going to a gym, but that became monotonous and lonely. I dove into my career, but I still felt dissatisfied with my life. Something was missing. The team atmosphere that I had experienced as a college athlete just wasn't there. I felt lost and alone. I wanted an activity and community that would push my physical and mental abilities and fill that big void in my life.

After a year of soul-searching, I did a little internet research and voila! The Dominion Derby Girls were recruiting! I shot a quick introductory email to the "Fresh Meat Committee" and got their practice schedule. When I went to watch a practice, I immediately fell in love. Women of every variation — size, age, career, ethnicity, and sexual orientation — were on the rink and skating their hearts out! They were smiling! They were sweating! Most of all, they were a team. I immediately ran to the local sports store to buy protective gear and skates. I couldn't wait for the next morning and my first practice as a derby girl!

Let me just say that my first practice was not pretty. My skating skills were probably about as good as Bambi on ice. But the coaches were great. They taught me the skills, and I became more and more confident on eight wheels. Within four months, I passed the skills and safety assessment and became competition-eligible.

My first bout was incredible. The feeling of nervousness mixed with excitement was overwhelming! After donning my uniform and my pigtail braids, I grabbed my gear and headed off, not knowing what was in store for me. Warming up, I felt my nerves fray. The other team wasn't intimidating me — it was the unnerving doubt in my abilities and the fear of letting my own teammates down.

Before I knew it, introductions started and the announcers were calling my name. "Number 36 AA, PIPPPPPYYYY LOOOOOONGSTALKER!"

Oh no! What do I do? I quickly raised my arms and blew a kiss to the crowd. I had the biggest grin on my face. This is it! My first bout! My debut as a Dominion Derby Girl! And then, the whistles blew, and the skating started. A sense of determination came over me. I would not let my teammates down. I would not use my inexperience as an excuse. This was a new period and a chance of redemption.

Lining up on the inside behind my pivot, The Ruffian, I looked around and realized the opposing team wasn't any different from me. They weren't any better than me. We all had eight wheels strapped to our feet. I would not let nerves get in my way. Then, the whistles blew. Off we went. All I could think was, "Stay together. Hold the line. Hit them HARD!" Then it happened. Their jammer was coming through the pack! I pushed off and skated straight into the path I knew she would take and WHACK! My shoulder went straight into her chest. Take that! That's right! A newbie just knocked you down!

What happened in that first period is a blur. Half-time came and went. A wave of confidence and pride came over me. I did it! It doesn't matter how good another skater is, as long as I remember what my coaches are teaching me and I put it to use. I can succeed in this sport! I can help my team! The rest of the period played out, and it was over too soon, but I will never forget that first hit. In every bout I skate in, I remember that initial rush of adrenaline and emotion that flooded over me.

Less than a year after stepping out onto the rink with unsteady feet at my first practice, I filled that empty void in my life. My teammates are my new family wherever life takes me. My skates have propelled me into a world that I could never have imagined existing. When I step out in my skates, I am transformed into a fearless woman with the confidence and agility that I never thought I'd possess. I am a stronger woman because of roller derby, not just physically, but emotionally and mentally.

Pippy Longstalker was born in Washington state and currently lives in Northern Virginia. She earned her Bachelor's degree in music, was a veterinary assistant, and is a military wife and mother. Since 2009, she has skated with more than a half-dozen teams on different tracks with varying rulesets and has competed and medaled at national and international championships.

A prompt from Pippy: Find your nearest skating rink and roller derby league and put some time in on wheels. Whether it's to compete, dance, make friendships, or just let loose, being on wheels is an incredibly freeing experience!

Is there another sport or activity that you think would be loads of fun, but haven't yet dared to try? Take 15 minutes to look up gyms, recreational teams, or training opportunities nearby. Write down what you find and schedule an introductory visit.

"The one thing I do not want to be called is First Lady. It sounds like a saddle horse."

~ Jacqueline Kennedy Onassis

Mrs. Spook

My husband Frank was an undercover officer for the CIA. The first foreign station of his career was in Spain, where we moved our family in 1965.

Once, there was an intriguing assignment for me. Frank had been meeting with a Spanish-speaking Russian (Boris) who was being highly paid for his information by the CIA. Frank was suspicious that Boris was a double agent, working both sides, as it were, so he asked for my help one evening. The plan was as follows: Boris would have coffee in a small café, taking a seat by the window where Frank could see him. Frank would then drive by the café in a particular Volkswagen. When Boris spotted the car going by, he would walk to a designated corner several blocks away and Frank would pick him up there.

When Boris exited the café, I was to walk a discreet distance behind, keeping a keen eye on him. I was to wear a black wig (which I borrowed from a friend "for a costume party") and an ankle-length brown coat. I would also carry a large, black umbrella, which I would use like a walking stick. If Boris talked to anyone on the street or made a phone call, I was to open the umbrella to signal Frank. This, of course, was a really sappy piece of drama, in my opinion.

Frank was carrying a German passport and wore a fake mustache and thick glasses, as he did every time he'd met with Boris. When we drove away from our house in the Volkswagen, he said he wasn't feeling well. I suggested it was just nerves, or perhaps the thick glasses. A few minutes later, Frank shot his head out the window and vomited violently. This was not a good beginning, I thought. Definitely not good.

The café where we were to see Boris was on an intimate little street in a residential area. We parked nearby. Frank got out of the car with me and we sat on a bench so he could catch his breath. He threw up again. "Put your head down!" I ordered heartlessly, as though I were annoyed with him. I also ducked my head, thinking one of us might be recognized. I realized I was looking at the puddle of Frank's upheaval and his mustache was in it. I quickly picked up the mustache and slapped it on Frank's ashen upper lip, but it wouldn't stick. Half of it did, but the other half didn't. It hung down to his chin.

Boris wasn't by the café window yet. I could see a *farmacia* (pharmacy) sign across the way, so I bolted across the street, my long brown coat billowing behind me. Mission: adhesive tape. I quickly bought the tape and ran back. Folding the tape over, I was able to jam Frank's mustache back in place. He was so sick by now that he was trembling. He glanced up and raised his eyebrows. There was Boris in the café. Frank stood, staggered over to the Volkswagen and pulled away.

I waited until Boris left the café, and then followed at a distance. It was a clear evening, filled with stars; the big, black umbrella was a ludicrous accessory and would look even crazier if I opened it. Boris lit a cigarette and strolled down the street. He spoke to no one. I was not destined to be Mary Poppins tonight. After he got in the Volkswagen with Frank, I hailed a taxi to go home, removing my wig and coat to avoid suspicion when I arrived. The driver seemed to find this only mildly interesting. (We had donned our gay apparel in the garage before we left).

Frank's plan after picking up Boris was to go to a room in a very large and busy hotel. They would have their discussion there, as they had done on previous occasions. Earlier in the day, after booking the room with his German passport, Frank had rigged a reel-to-reel tape recorder behind the bed. (There was nothing simpler at that time). He later told me that when they got to the hotel room, he was imploding with diarrhea and had to apologize to Boris for his non-stop trips to the bathroom. As he sat on the toilet, he imagined the whir-r-r-r of the tape and the impending doom if it reached an end and began to flap.

There was no way of turning the tape machine off without moving the bed and he was becoming concerned. There was only one thing to do. He had to tell Boris how ill he was and arrange to meet him another time. Luckily, Boris had a written report to give him and didn't mind rescheduling their discussion. A soon as the door closed behind him, the tape started to flap.

Frank spent the following week in bed with stomach flu and high fever. Shaken, but not stirred.

Lillian McCloy was the wife of a deep undercover CIA officer during the Cold War. This story is an excerpt from her memoir, Six Car Lengths Behind an Elephant, *which was published when she was 90 years old. John le Carré describes the book as "a charming and unusual portrait of the secret life."*

Have you ever pretended to be someone else in a real-life situation, without ever revealing your true identity? Have you worn a costume (and it wasn't a costume party) or used a fake accent? When and why? And if you haven't, imagine a scene where you do.

"'What is courage?' I ask.
'Bearing witness. That is a form of courage.'"

~ Jessica Stern

JO-ANNE MCARTHUR

Love Made Visible

It's summer in the Antarctic and on sunny days I can venture out onto the bow of our Sea Shepherd vessel, the *Bob Barker,* to let the warmth penetrate my bones. Between chores, the bow is a great place to spend a bit of idle time outdoors reflecting on life and on our mission here in the southern oceans.

Keep a sharp eye and you'll spy dolphins, penguins, albatross, and southern petrels. These moments of quietude give me time to reflect on how the heck I got to be on this boat of environmental and animal rights activists, and on how a few defining life decisions led me to this moment.

Life won't always be this idyllic aboard our boat, which the crew affectionately refers to as *"The Bob."* We will have intensely dangerous confrontations with our rivals, the Japanese whaling fleet. Our boat is one of three on this 2009-2010 Antarctic Mission to stop the poaching of up to 935 minke whales which are hunted by the fleet and sold for meat in Japan.

The hunt occurs under the thin guise of "research" — a word which is painted in English on the side of their processing ship, no less — and though the member countries of the International Whaling Commission have imposed a ban on whaling in this southern sanctuary, no one is there to enforce the ban. Long-time animal activist Paul Watson decided to take the matter into his own hands, sending ships down to the Antarctic to intercept the slaughter of these endangered animals.

My title on board *The Bob* is "Sea Shepherd Crew Photographer." It's a role I almost turned down in lieu of a much-needed restful winter in Canada. When I think about a "fabulous" experience or moment in my life, the story of how I came to be on *The Bob* is one of those. I am a photojournalist and the work I do for animal rights is rewarding and exhausting.

The year 2009 was undoubtedly one of the craziest of my 30-odd years. It began with a trip through Guatemala and Belize, followed by three months in Africa. While shooting a photo story at a primate sanctuary in Cameroon, I contracted dengue fever, which left my body crippled with reactive arthritis. Refusing to return home for a rest, I moved on to Uganda to work with the Jane Goodall Institute. There, I asked a doctor to load me up with the meds necessary to allow me to continue my work. These meds were steroids, and I relied on them for close to four months. They helped me to walk and work, but slowed my overall healing significantly.

After a brief rest in Canada, I left for Spain and France to do factory farm investigations and a story about the brutal slaying of bulls during *La Corrida*. Night after night, with cameras in hand, I travelled all over the country with the animal advocacy organization Animal Equality, to document the extreme suffering of pigs, chickens, egg-laying hens, and bulls. From there I went on to Scandinavia, where I documented mink farming with the Swedish organization Djurattsalliansen. It was exhausting work, both physically and emotionally. The travelling and all-night investigative escapades left me drained in a profound way.

I do all this investigative work so that I can help expose the use and abuse of animals worldwide. The images I take have become part of my umbrella project on the subject matter, called *We Animals*, and over one hundred animal welfare organizations have used my images to promote their work. *We Animals* is my passions combined: my love for story-telling through the lens and my love for helping animals, seamlessly entwined, epitomizing that famous quote by the writer Kahlil Gibran, "Work is love made visible." I feel strongly that my work for *We Animals* is what I was born to do. I certainly exemplified this when I wrote to Sea Shepherd that November.

The Sea Shepherd mission was on the heels of my European investigative work, so I put off replying to their email asking me whether I'd like to come on board and join the crew. The opportunity stood before me as a chance of a lifetime: saving whales, visiting the Antarctic, living on a boat, working alongside other dedicated activists . . . incredible! Yet I knew that I had to say no for the sake of my recovering health and my sanity. I wrote a carefully crafted email saying that I would love to join future campaigns, but would regretfully decline this upcoming mission. I sat there at my computer before hitting "send," feeling responsible but hollow. As I navigated my mouse to the "send" button, however, I changed my mind. Deleting the email, with a smile and a sigh, I wrote the words "Sign me up!" and hit "send." My fate was sealed.

My "yes" to Sea Shepherd was a door thrown open wide. I felt like I was staring down a dark abyss of danger, seasickness, and further sleep deprivation. It was all that and so much more. Not only did I have the adventure of a lifetime with inspiring activists and work that was meaningful to me, but my photos were also published by over two thousand news agencies worldwide. Though I was working for Sea Shepherd for free, it turned out to be a decent career move, while helping to expose the poaching of whales in the southern oceans. I'm also happy to report that my Sea Shepherd mission only somewhat slowed my recovery to full health. The dengue-induced arthritis lingered, but I have made close to a full recovery.

When I finally caught my breath after that whirlwind twelve months, I was sure that things would slow down and that there'd be calmer waters ahead. That whirlwind hasn't really stopped. Since that year, I have travelled to dozens more countries and worked with many inspiring animal protection groups to document factory farms, wildlife sanctuaries, puppy mills, captive animals, fur farms, slaughterhouse vigils, animal fairs, and more. I have written two books and, with Dr. Keri Cronin, launched the Unbound Project to highlight the work of women on the front lines of animal advocacy. Little did I know that in 2009, I was just getting started.

In documenting our complex relationships with animals, I see the best and worst of humanity: the willingness of so many to look the other way in the face of atrocities, and the refusal of some to turn away.

The work I do is difficult and devastating. As I write this in 2015, I've shed more tears than I thought possible over the cruelty, hopelessness, and apathy that I have witnessed. Not being able to save the tens of thousands of animals I've met causes me a lot of heartache too. Yet every moment of injustice and suffering that I have captured serves a purpose. My images have been presented to government committees examining industry practices. They have been mounted on billboards that are seen by millions of people. They have been featured in countless exposés highlighting practices that would otherwise remain in the dark. The work is hard, yes, but the suffering of those animals is not lessened by our not seeing it. Change will only come with visibility, so I continue my work to make sure these beings are seen.

On the other side of what I do are the rescued animals. And the activists who give — and risk — everything to make sure that those animals know that, despite everything they have been through, they're safe now. They're loved. My work for animals is my love made visible.

Jo-Anne McArthur is an award-winning animal photojournalist, author, educator, and the founder of We Animals Media, a photo agency which explores our uses, abuses, and sharing of spaces with the animals of this planet. She is the protagonist in the award-winning documentary The Ghosts in Our Machine *(2013) and has authored three books,* We Animals *(2013),* Captive *(2017) and* HIDDEN: Animals in the Anthropocene *(2020). We Animals Media makes thousands of images and videos available for free to anyone advocating for animals.*

A prompt from Jo-Anne: I have three simple words affixed to my office wall: "Begin It Now." I think it's great life advice for those of us who want to be the change we wish to see in the world. What important life goal do you have languishing on a back burner? Begin It Now!

"I'd rather regret the risks that didn't work out than the chances I didn't take at all."

~ Simone Biles

PENNY ROSS BURK

Fear City

The traffic going up Route 81 was a little heavy, but pride kept me on the highway and passionately directed. I was scared to death, an introvert trying to function in an extrovert's world, flying down the road and heading towards a destination almost too frightening to talk about.

After a recent divorce and a very quiet spring, I decided to challenge my still winterized mind and body to an impromptu trip to New York City with my two kids. It represented some of my worst fears, ones that my ex-husband previously alleviated by taking complete control. For the past ten years he was the one to drive in the city, find parking, ward off strangers, negotiate the subway, and pay for everything along the way. This left me with the awesome responsibility of, well, tagging along.

Over the years I had become totally dependent on him and now that he was gone, I spent the entire winter and spring immobilized by my fears. I had to get out of the house! Cabin fever was setting in, and I wanted to see my dear aunt and uncle. We lived a solid five hours from them and they lived in the heart of (tremble, shudder) mid-town Manhattan.

Monday night, Uncle Milt called to announce his departure from the city to his retreat in Maine where he and Aunt Molly spent their summers. "But Milt!" I complained, "I really want to see you, it's been ages!"

"So, come up," he answered.

"That's it, come up? We would have to leave . . ." (pausing to check the calendar and then panicking) . . . "tomorrow!"

I heard Molly snickering in the background, "She won't make it. She's stuck in the country without a man. She couldn't even make it to Maine last year without him!" That did it! "Milt, I'll call you before I leave." I slammed the phone down while I cursed Molly for knowing how to push all my buttons.

I searched frantically for reasons not to go, but couldn't blame a single illness, gas shortage, or flat tire. But, just because that's the way the cookie crumbles (especially in the back seat of our car), we found ourselves hurtling down the highway into the unknown.

The children quietly watched Mommy from the back of the van while she strangled the steering wheel with pale-white knuckles. "It'll be fine," I repeatedly told myself while periodically looking over my shoulder at the kids. "Hey guys, don't look so scared. It'll be fine, it'll be fine, it'll be fine."

Pennsylvania was okay, and to my surprise New Jersey wasn't too bad either. Even the dreaded New Jersey Turnpike offered no obstacles. There was hardly anyone on the road and my eight-year-old daughter noted the color coming back into my hands. We were three exits away from where we needed to be, but for me, the tough part was still coming up.

The Holland Tunnel looked like any other tunnel, but being in a paranoid state of mind, I imagined it turning into a giant, spiraling board going much deeper than the harbor and of course, never ending. The other side scared me even more.

What happens if I get a case of amnesia and forget which way to go? Or no doubt, I'll get cut off and miss my turn and be lost, driving in circles forever. And then, I'll get accosted by some psycho-killer just waiting for a mom with two kids from West Virginia to attack.

That last thought got to me. "Lock the doors, guys."

"But Mom, we're only four blocks away!"

"I don't care, lock 'em anyway!"

For some mysterious reason, the garage was right where we left it one year earlier and hadn't been replaced by a skyscraper or 12 new one-way streets. We had arrived, with no wrong turns and without the use of husbands, boyfriends, or any other adults.

Now, if we could make it to Milt and Molly's storefront apartment, schlepping pillows, clothes, stuffed animals, and five ears of corn, life would be perfect. To my amazement, one foot fell in front of the other and in no time, I was a functioning, independent person knocking on my aunt and uncle's door.

After hugs of greeting and surprise at the great time we made driving up, we talked briefly about family, dinner, and our plans for the next day. In order to get the kids to go along so easily, I had to bribe them with a visit to the Statue of Liberty. My four-year-old son called it the Statue of Levity and couldn't wait to go. As we sat around discussing plans, I cheerfully asked who was going to go with us. Molly said she would be at the dentist and had other appointments through the day. Milt immediately said, "No," not even waiting for Molly to finish listing her excuses.

"You mean no one will go with us?" I was beginning to panic (again). There was no way out of this one. I had promised the kids. Of course, we just had to go by subway, otherwise known (at least to me) as the underground-snake-maze-from-hell, which devours innocent country people like us. I was trapped.

Milt and Molly told us where to go and when to transfer. Transfer? Oh great, the snake pit maze was going to swallow us whole and we'd never come out again, except as raving, drooling, mad people with torn clothes and matted hair.

"Then what, Milt? I didn't hear what you said. You're not sure of the stop? Not sure of the stop!?"

Could it get any worse?

"You mean I'll have to look at a map, which I won't understand because they're all written in a foreign language? And then I'll have to ask a New Yorker who will sneer at me and speak really fast, and if I ask him to repeat the answer, will knife me?"

"Bowling Green, Molly? What's that? You mean the subway doesn't go right to the ferry? We'll have to walk through Battery Park . . ." (major freak out) . . . "with the kids?"

Swallowing became an audible event, and my heart quickly sank into my stomach. "Is there any other way?" I asked hopefully.

"Sure, the bus on Broadway goes right there."

"You're kidding," (visible relief). "Did you hear that, kids? We'll be able to see everything — above ground!"

"We want the train — we want the train!"

Milt and Molly were already discussing eggplant lasagna at Ray's Restaurant for dinner while I slid deep into my chair, wondering if I could feign some illness like irreversible brain damage. I ate lightly, and finally decided this looked exactly like the kind of fear that needed to be faced head-on. Okay, I'll do it, I thought, if we wind up in Newark then I'll never have to mow the lawn again. Sounds good to me, I told myself, and made the deal.

The next morning, I asked the kids again, just to make sure, if maybe we should stay with Milt and Molly for the day. "No" was the simultaneous answer. The directions were repeated for the emotionally and directionally challenged, the front door opened, and there it was, the kind of concrete that nightmares were made of.

"Bus, right, guys?"

"We want the train, we want the train."

"Okay, okay."

I don't know what happened; there must have been some happy gas sprayed in the tunnels the night before. The token man smiled and a lady showed us where to transfer. In Bowling Green, the sky was blue and the sun was shining, as it had been when we started.

I was beginning to get the hang of this: adult; two legs; two eyes; most of a brain. Hey, no problem, I could do this in daylight. Did it matter that my daughter complained she had no more circulation in the hand I was holding?

The Statue of Levity was filled with people like myself who really did speak foreign languages. I was ready to help, if asked.

"Okay, guys, you've seen the statue. Now let's go explore!"

"Can't we just go back to Uncle Milt and Aunt Molly's?"

"Sure, let's take a different uptown train."

"We want to take a cab."

"Forget it, it's cheaper to take the subway."

Did I just say that? I went through the bowels of the city and came through unscathed. In fact, I was feeling more confident than I had in years.

Back at the apartment, the sun was setting on a beautiful summer day in the most exciting city in the world. As I thought about the day, I got around to reminding myself that I grew up around here. I know the city pretty well. I walked the length of the island once many years ago and in the middle of the night! Yeah, I used to hang out in Washington Square Park and St. Marks Place back in the late '60s. We were up in Harlem once and...

It's amazing how I'd finally grown up enough to be as independent as I was 30 years ago.

Penny Ross Burk is an artist/writer living in the Northern Virginia area. She has worked for many years in the film and TV industry, which serves to keep her art alive.

Are there any "everyday" types of tasks/activities that feel daring to do solo, because you're used to someone else doing them *for* you . . . or *with* you? Driving a long distance? Cooking a big meal? Managing a particular household chore? Taking public transit in an unfamiliar city? Speaking another language?

"'Why the fuck not me?'
should be your motto."

~ Mindy Kaling

SIMON CHAITOWITZ

Playing the Cancer Card

Some clouds have some surprisingly useful silver linings. Cancer, for example.

No, I'm not one of those cheery and "oh so brave" sick people who thinks that cancer made me a better person or helped me find my true self. I hate cancer. I'm pissed I got it the first time and even more mad I got it a second time (an unfortunate little side effect of treatment from the first one).

So no, I'm not into pretending that cancer isn't horrible. But the Big C does have one little perk that doesn't get publicized much. And I'd like to make sure that cancer "survivors" don't guilt-trip themselves out of using it. (Like yours truly, until recently.)

What I'm talking about is taking advantage of any possible opportunity you have to do what you want and not do what you don't want. For example, if you're immune suppressed, the doctors tell you to quit cleaning litter boxes, changing diapers, taking out the garbage, or weeding gardens (yes, yes, yes, and yes!) but there are tons more Get Out of Jail Free Cards just waiting to be picked up.

In other words, don't feel shy about using cancer to your own ends — whether that's making your life better, furthering your cause, or just helping yourself get through the day. I call it "Playing the Cancer

Card." Kristin Boles, a cancer listserv mate, says she and her husband call it the "Fringe Benefits of Cancer."

Here are just a few examples. All are either based on my experiences or those of other cancer survivors:

- Get out of a parking ticket. Write a nice letter to the city explaining how you were rushing to your CANCER appointment when you noticed the meter you chose wasn't working. Voila! Fee waived.

- Talk your way into meetings with secretaries of state and the prime minister. Adrian Sudbury, an advocate for bone marrow donation in England, says his disease regularly opens doors for him. Brilliant.

- Skip long, boring events. No need to feel obligated to attend that dreaded yearly family reunion if you don't enjoy it. You need your rest, after all. But if you find yourself at the event, and just can't take it anymore, no worries. No one will take your departure personally.

- Get discounts at nice hotels. No kidding. The last time I went out of town for a check-up, I found out that one of my favorite hotels offered a 20 percent discount to guests visiting the nearby clinics. It's easier to justify luxury with that kind of savings.

- See your words in print. If there's one phrase that virtually guarantees you'll make it onto the Letters to the Editor page, it's "As a cancer survivor, I feel . . ." Nearly every letter I've started like that has been published. The Letters page is a great place to share your ideas about doctors, the pharmaceutical industry, or anything else related to cancer. (Of course, if you're already famous, you can probably use cancer to get yourself on a show like *Larry King*.)

Those of us who are immune-suppressed have even more built-in excuses. One woman just told me she talked her way into the use of an indoor bathroom at a summer festival where everyone else had to use the portable toilets. Two points for creativity and boldness! (Disclosure: Sometimes I'm still too chicken to ask to be the first in the buffet line.)

Those of us who are genetically disposed to guilt complexes may have an extra hard time following this advice. But trust me.

When life hands you cancer, this is your chance to eat dessert first, stop shaving your legs, switch to part-time work, or get out of jury duty. Whatever you want, whenever you want it. Go for it.

Simon Chaitowitz was a writer and two-time cancer survivor who lived and worked in Washington, D.C. As much as she disliked the word "survivor," she admitted it could be useful. Simon passed away less than one year after contributing this story to Dare to be Fabulous. *She died from a blood disorder caused by the treatment she underwent for breast cancer.*

Do you have a disease or a disability? Describe three scenarios where you could (or do) "play that card" in order to benefit from a situation.

"I am an endangered species
But I sing no victim's song
I am a woman I am an artist
And I know where my voice belongs
I know where my soul belongs
I know where I belong."

~ Dianne Reeves

TERRI LYNE CARRINGTON

Full Circle and Living an Authentic Life

When I look back on my life, there are a lot of instances where people, especially women, have told me how much I inspire them, seeing me as fearless and daring. This was not always comfortable, because I always felt like I was just being me. Factually speaking, I am a drummer, playing an instrument predominantly played by men in a male-dominated music industry, so I have had to be fearless and daring or I would not have gotten very far in my field. What I find interesting is how I have needed to present myself in order to be accepted in this community. This was not a fully conscious effort on my part.

I was always pretty good at reading personalities and figuring out what needed to be done or said for a situation to produce or fulfill its maximum potential. My personality is strong, which is not uncommon for women in my field, and people often found me to be intimidating, so I developed a way to present a softened version of myself — a "me" that I actually grew to be quite fond of. Still, what repeatedly rings in my ears is my mother's voice scolding me as a child for being too concerned with what other people think. And later in life, I recall my dad's voice remarking on how it was the veteran musicians — one or two generations before mine — that hired and supported me the most, indicating that I was never fully accepted by the majority of my peers. To be noted, I was nearly peerless on my instrument.

During that period when I worked mostly with musicians of a previous generation, I learned more than I could have ever imagined had they not mentored me. People like Jack DeJohnette, Clark Terry, Wayne Shorter, Lester Bowie, Herbie Hancock, Bernice Johnson Reagon, as well as my big sister-friends that were hovering around 10 years my senior: Dianne Reeves, Patrice Rushen, Cassandra Wilson. All these people helped to create a nurturing community that I called home, literally and figuratively. I was able to be open, honest and a work-in-progress, while still trying to figure out how I fit into the dynamic of the male-centered jazz culture.

As I matured, I discovered that a big part of the "me" that had developed was for the comfort of others. I toed the line between what would be considered acceptable social behavior for women in the '80s and '90s, and the far less acceptable behavior of a woman that wanted the same societal freedoms of her male counterparts. It was a balancing act that often became tiresome. Now that I'm in my 50s, as cliché as it may sound, I am finally daring to be my fabulous self, however that turns out, and without regard for others' expectations.

I am finally realizing how much time I wasted trying to fit into various boxes — from worrying about who likes me, or who doesn't, to worrying about my pant size or my hairstyle. Dianne Reeves once told me that I spent too much time trying to find "what is hip?" and that I did not realize that I *am* "what is hip!" I thought about that one day and the truth in her statement brought me to tears. Though I am confident, intelligent, strong-willed, and relatively outspoken, I have felt very misunderstood over the course of my life. I finally get that I hold some responsibility for that. I see that it takes a lot of courage to discover and to be your authentic self in an environment that is constantly telling you how to be.

I know now that the freedom I've been looking for has always been possible, and that I have been my own roadblock to fully accessing it. This kind of freedom resides within. I still struggle to bring it to the exterior, but I know that I have to in order to live my life genuinely. It is not something that someone else will grant me.

Many examples in my life have brought these principles to light for me. When I tried to make an album after the success of my Grammy-nominated debut album in 1989, I could not get any interest. I went on for over 10 years without label interest, but when I invested in myself, produced and paid for it on my own, my career trajectory transformed to becoming a solo artist who has since won three Grammy Awards, creating the art autonomously.

When it comes to producing records, I think that there is, in fact, a glass ceiling for me. No matter how many Grammys I win for my productions, very few people ask me to produce for them. And when I heard about some of the budgets that well-known male producers get, I quickly realized the gap in my financial accommodation versus theirs.

I've played with the greatest musicians in jazz, and I'm not sure if I was getting paid equitably with my male counterparts, but I didn't sense as much of a glass ceiling as a musician. Or maybe I was a part of breaking it. Every time I play, it still seems like someone is surprised by my ability. That is probably the biggest thing that reminds me of how, systemically, we are all products of patriarchy.

Over the years, I recall Angela Davis telling me how I sounded like "one of the guys" when I talked about women musicians. I didn't realize what she meant until more recently, when I became sensitive to gender inequities in jazz. Basically, I sounded like a woman that was okay with how everything had been, because I had a thriving career. I was a product of patriarchy and did not see how I was also contributing to it.

Of course, this has changed. I check in with myself all the time to keep myself honest. And though my sound has not really changed, I am more accepting of my own playing style. I don't feel like I have to hit the drums as hard, or that I need to prove anything.

With all the praise, awards, and critical acclaim I have received over the years, outward reinforcement of my being "fabulous" never really stuck with me because career accomplishments alone did not make me feel complete. It is my personal growth and discovery of self that makes me feel more fabulous every year, and contributes heavily to my faith, confidence, and perseverance. Without these things, I could not successfully pass my knowledge and experience on to others.

The one thing that has made me feel especially fabulous is my decision to raise a child, which has now been a 16-year journey. Having a child, something that is simple for (or even expected of) many women, has presented its challenges, but I would not trade the experience for anything in the world. It takes work, sacrifice, and commitment to adapt — regularly. I had romanticized parenthood, but now I see how fabulous mothers truly are. It is the hardest thing I have ever done! Although co-parenting is not always easy, we are both grateful and proud to be parents to an amazing boy. I had faith that the right "child spirit" would choose us, and I still believe that to be true. Though my family is being formed alternatively, there is a natural joy and sense of purpose that comes with this, and I am so glad I did not allow the business of my career to rob me of this experience.

I am now the Founder and Artistic Director of the Berklee Institute of Jazz and Gender Justice, so my life has come full circle, teaching at the same college I attended over 30 years ago. I moved back to my hometown ten years ago, and I am far away from everything I knew and loved in Southern California, but this chapter is still being written and I know the universe will unfold the future, as it should. I'm in my 50s and, as cliché as it may seem, I am finally daring to be my fabulous self, however that turns out, and without regard for others' expectations.

Terri Lyne Carrington was given her first set of drums at the age of seven. By the age of 11, she received a full scholarship to the prestigious Berklee College of Music. She has toured with Herbie Hancock, Wayne Shorter, Stan Getz, Al Jarreau and others. She is also a three-time GRAMMY award-winning artist and producer. She is also the Founder and Artistic Director of the Berklee Institute of Jazz and Gender Justice.

A prompt from Terri Lyne: Are you surprised to see women shredding on electric guitar or ripping away at the drums? Do you gender instruments, thinking flute or violin or piano are for women and trumpet or percussion are for men? How else do gender roles affect your listening? How many women instrumentalists do you have in your music collection?

"I always wanted to be somebody.
If I made it, it's half because I was game enough
to take a lot of punishment along the way
and half because there were a lot of people
who cared enough to help me."

~ Althea Gibson

On the Edge

On May 24, 2010, I made it to the summit of Mount Everest. I had a haunting history with that mountain. After turning back just a few hundred feet from the top in 2002 due to crap weather and poor visibility — I swore I would never try again. And trust me, there were many moments of self-doubt on my second attempt as my previous expedition was such a high-profile failure. Because we were the first American Women's Everest expedition, we had a ton of media coverage. All of the major news outlets were following our climb . . . AND THEN WE DIDN'T MAKE IT. Upon our return, we had to do dozens of TV interviews and talk about what happened. It felt like a punch in the gut because everyone was so focused on the fact that we didn't make it. No one seemed to care that we were the first team of American women to even try something like this, and it was an altitude record for every member of my team. All anyone could talk about was the fact that we did not achieve our goal of reaching the summit. We were even the butt of Jay Leno's opening monologue joke. Ouch. I had to overcome an extreme fear of failure in order to get up my guts to go back again. That fear of failure felt greater than the fear of getting hurt or dying on Everest.

I am often asked what it was like — to go back to that mountain eight years later, after everything I had been through, and finally stand on top of the highest mountain in the world. I can honestly tell you (wait for it . . . deep breath . . .) it just wasn't that big a deal. Heavy sigh. Think about it for a moment. It's just a mountain. It's nothing more than a big ol' pile of rock and ice. And you are only on the summit for a very short time. You spend two months climbing that mountain, and only a few minutes at the very top. I was up there for thirty minutes. Standing on top of a mountain is not important, and the people who stand on top of Mount Everest are no better than the people who turn around short of the summit. Because climbing mountains isn't about standing on the top of a pile of rock and ice for a few minutes — it's about the lessons you learn along the way and how you are going to use that knowledge and experience to better yourself going forward.

I promise you that plenty of better, stronger, more skilled, much more deserving climbers than Alison Levine didn't make it that day — for whatever reason. Most of them turned back because of the weather. But because I had that failed experience from 2002 under my belt, I knew what it felt like to get beat up and knocked around on that mountain. I knew what it was like to get the snot kicked out of me high up on the summit ridge in a storm. And I wasn't afraid of that this time around. I knew what my risk tolerance was, and I knew what my pain threshold was. Had I not had that failed experience eight years prior, I very well might have turned around when most others did.

Shortly after my return, the *New York Times* published a photo of me at the summit, which resulted in phone calls from dozens of friends congratulating me on the accomplishment. But there was a lot more to that photo than what they could see. Let me tell you what they didn't see: the sponsors who helped to fund my trip, the logistics providers who got all the permits in order, the amazing team of Sherpas who helped ferry loads up and down the mountain, the incredible guides who gave me direction along the way, the friends who helped me train before I left for Nepal, the loved ones who gave me their moral support leading up to the trip . . . I could go on. Always remember: nobody gets to the top of Mount Everest by themselves. Nobody.

Alison Levine is a history-making polar explorer and mountaineer. She has climbed the highest peak on every continent, served as the team captain of the first American Women's Everest Expedition, and skied to both the North and South Poles. She is the author of the NY Times *bestseller,* On the Edge, *and is the executive producer of the documentary film,* PASANG: In the Shadow of Everest.

What have you achieved that you could not possibly have done without the help of others? List all the people, and the ways they helped make your achievement possible.

"In art and dream may you proceed with abandon. In life may you proceed with balance and stealth."

~ Patti Smith

I Canceled My Wedding

When I was 24, I canceled my wedding ten days before it was to happen. For many years, it was hard for me to talk about. Whenever it came up, people would generally express enthusiastic support or sympathy and I'd smile slightly to show appreciation, but internally, I was wincing. It took more than ten years to get over my feelings of shame and guilt. It took me that long to look back on my actions with any amount of objectivity or compassion.

Mark was my first boyfriend. He was adorable, quirky, fun. I fell in love with him when I was a sophomore at Duke. He had just graduated and was unsure about which career he wanted to pursue, so he continued working at his former summer job as a big rig driver with a local moving company. I think he'd concur that our shared adventures in that 18-wheeler were probably the highlight of our relationship.

Three years later, when I was one year out of college, Mark was accepted at the McGeorge School of Law in Sacramento, so we moved to California. At the new student orientation, one of the speakers offered the depressing statistic that most couples at the onset of law school are unlikely to stay together through graduation. We looked at each other; "not us," we scoffed. A few months later, we were engaged.

While Mark attended law classes during the day, I worked at a children's theatre company. While he studied diligently every night, I attended rehearsals for roles I landed in local theatre productions. As I re-discovered creative expression through acting, Mark immersed himself in facts, logic, and argument. His quirky humor and adventurous spirit began to give way to a more stoic and serious demeanor.

I knew the rigors of law school were tough, so I tried to provide him with support and encouragement. Yet, I felt restless. I yearned to expand and explore. I shared few of my own day-to-day experiences with Mark, because law school was all-consuming. If he wasn't in class, he was in the library or with a study group. Weekends were no different. I barely saw him. He'd apologize for his distracted state and his full-throttle focus on the law, and I'd tell him that I understood.

I could make excuses about our situation being temporary, but at the same time, I felt like our paths were becoming more and more divergent. I'd been determined to support him, but now I was wondering, what about me? I began to feel like two people: my old, predictable self with Mark, and my new, growing self in his absence. I began thinking about the fact that he was my first and only boyfriend, that we were still young and finding our way. I loved him, but getting married suddenly felt like a bad idea.

Our wedding day was fast approaching. Plans had been made and guests invited. I felt queasy and riddled with fear. He'd been my everything for five solid years. What was I going to do? For the first time since we'd been together, I felt utterly alone, facing the world and my life head-on. I felt like I was living in a thick, gray fog of foreboding.

Two weeks before the wedding, I called my mother. When she asked me how I was feeling as the wedding approached, I tried to lightly express my feelings of apprehension, as if they were probably normal or not to be taken too seriously. She immediately got to the heart of the matter. She made it simple and practical and real. "This is your life, Johanna," she said. "You need to do what your heart dictates. It'll be fine. You'll be fine. Don't go through with it if you're not ready." Her sympathetic and loving tone touched me deeply. Then, she dared to present the option of a cancellation, as if it wasn't a big deal. "It's only money," she said. "I think I can get deposits back, and if I don't, it's okay." Perhaps this was why I had called her in the first place; a sub-conscious need to get consent.

I'm kind of embarrassed to admit this, but I hadn't even thought about the deposits. These things were frankly the least of my concerns. The anxiety over possibly canceling our wedding had nothing to do with money or with canceling all the scheduled plans. I barely even thought about the guests. The only thing on my mind was Mark. How was I going to tell Mark? I was about to devastate the person I loved most. He had been my best friend for five years and now . . . what?

Time was ticking. Every time I pushed myself to say something, I felt sick to my stomach and could barely open my mouth to talk. The wedding was now *ten days away* and the pressure was overwhelming. I was swimming in so much anxiety that I couldn't eat. No one else was going to do this for me. I had to battle my overwhelming anxiety and speak up.

I pushed myself to speak after dinner one night. "How are you feeling about the wedding?" I asked, while we were washing dishes. My entire body was shaking, but I pretended to be calm. I was hoping he'd give me an easy out. "Fine," he replied matter-of-factly. He looked at me. "Why?" he asked. I felt woozy. I wanted to take several deep breaths, but I continued to control my voice and sound calm. "Oh, I guess I'm just having those feelings people talk about." And from there it went. Second by agonizing second.

"What feelings?" he asked. "You know, second thoughts. Fear. Haven't you had any?" I tried to ask innocently. "No," he said. He couldn't have made it any more difficult. A panicked conviction took over and I realized that I had to pounce right in. NOW OR NEVER.

I honestly don't recall what I said next. It's like when you're in an accident and you don't remember the moment of impact. I remember rambling and mumbling and trying to temper my beating heart until he finally asked me the question: "Do you want to call it off?" This is when my memory kicks back in. Like the moment after the accident, when you come to. "Yeah," I said, shaking, and now crying, apologetic.

He was calm. He did not get angry or turn inside himself and brood, which was more common for him. Remarkably, his focus was on my own well-being. I guess my agony was palpable.

We stayed up through the entire night. It felt like we were on a hallucinogenic drug or living in a twilight zone. Both of our emotions were raw. We talked, we cried, we chain smoked, we held each other. When I finally fell asleep just before dawn, Mark stayed up. I awoke a few hours later to see him kneeling before me with a breakfast tray holding a five-page letter, a plate of food, and flowers. In the letter, Mark expressed his deep love for me and beckoned for me to give him another chance. It was like beauty and pain blended in a horrible and exhilarating cocktail. The horrible feeling of knowing this man loved me so much, and the awareness that I was still going to call it off, was horrid. And you talk about courage. His letter was an act of love that I will never forget.

"I think we should still go to Durham," Mark said about the location where we were to wed. "The flight cancellation fee will be ridiculous. We might as well go. We can visit with my family. It'll be good." I couldn't believe that he thought this would be a good idea. The last thing I wanted to do was bring myself that close to the plans I'd canceled, to be around his family at such a vulnerable time. How could Mark consider it? I even wondered if I felt worse as the canceller than he did as the cancellee.

He was determined to keep his itinerary and fly to Durham, with or without me. I understood that he needed to be with his family, but I couldn't bear the pain of going along. Our friend's dad, a doctor, kindly offered to write a medical note to the airline (I don't recall what he wrote, something about an infection and not being able to fly), so I could avoid the cancellation fee for my ticket.

The flight was a red-eye. I drove Mark to the airport and parked in the lot, wanting to be by his side until the last possible minute. He took his small bag of clothes from the trunk and half-smiled as I closed it.

"There should be two of these," he said. I had been forcing the tears back, forcing the tears back, forcing the tears back through the drive there, but now, with those words uttered, I could do it no longer. He laughed a little when he realized how raw we both were, how difficult it was to find a way through this emotional process. We held hands and walked to the airline counter, where he presented both of our tickets and I presented my letter from the doctor. As the airline attendant read the letter, Mark looked at me. "You can still go," he whispered. I shook my head, not wanting the attendant to realize it was really an option.

The doctor's letter served its purpose and I got a voucher. Mark got a boarding pass. With fifteen minutes to spare before he had to board, we walked outside and leaned on a railing watching the planes in the dark beyond. He gave it one more shot. "Come," he said. "It'll be fine. Come." I kept shaking my head no. I began to cry again and the valves wouldn't close this time. We hugged our goodbyes and he turned to go inside and board the plane.

Alone, detached, I walked back to my car, acutely aware that this moment marked the start of a new chapter in my life. I started the engine, crying so hard now that I was gulping for air. I drove slowly onto the freeway, hoping to get a hold of myself. An airplane engine sounded in the black expanse above me and I looked out the window to see a blinking light in the sky. Maybe it was his plane, or maybe another. I tried to focus on driving, but I couldn't see the road in front of me through my heavy sobs, so I immediately pulled over to the shoulder of the freeway. It was 11:00pm on a weeknight and there were few cars on the road, but I felt safer there. It took more than ten minutes to get a hold of myself and start driving again.

A few weeks after that fateful night, I moved into my own apartment, and several months later, we officially broke up. I moved to Los Angeles to study acting with Sanford Meisner, and he graduated from law school and began working as an attorney. We dated other people, but we stayed in touch. We both came to realize how much we missed each other and how rare it is to find the kind of connection we'd had. We began talking on the phone more often. Then, we began to visit each other on the weekends. Another year later, over the phone

one night, he joked about becoming engaged again, and in a careless moment, I agreed. When I landed the role of Catherine in *A View from the Bridge* at Palm Springs Playhouse, we decided I'd move in with him, since he was now an attorney in Palm Desert and his place was just 20 minutes away.

It took no time to recognize that there we were again; him in his world of fact, proof, and precedent, and away during the days; and me in my world of emotion, creativity, and catharsis, away during the evenings. It occurred to me finally that what we had most in common now was the connection from our past. It was a very special and rare kind of connection, which I realized after dating other people, but those magical days in college and that time in our lives was the reason it took hold. Years and experiences had taken us in other directions. We'd each changed and grown; were no longer as in sync. Without any hesitation, I initiated the conversation about canceling our second engagement, and Mark again was calm in his response, though this time, he agreed.

We broke up for good then. I moved back to L.A. where I proceeded to make a living as an actor, and Mark eventually opened his own law practice. We remained in touch and occasionally talked on the phone. Once, when he was in L.A. on business, we met for lunch. I didn't feel comfortable telling him about my own love life, but he shared stories about the woman he was dating. He'd been seeing her for a while and I liked hearing that. I wanted him to be happy.

About a year after that, I got word from a mutual friend that Mark had eloped. Just hearing that news felt like heavy sandbags of shame toppling off my shoulders. Within mere seconds, I was breathing easier and standing taller. It was as if I'd been holding my breath all that time. (Mark later told me how it happened: one sunny afternoon while they were working on their garden, his girlfriend dared him to get married, and he took the dare, driving her straight to the courthouse. This happened on October 16, he told me. My birthday.)

People tend to respond to my canceled wedding story with a congratulatory tone. A surprising number of married people have also added, "I wish I'd done that." It's shocking to hear that said so plainly and so often. Talk about a reality check: evidence that my act of canceling had served as a powerful, pre-emptive strike.

Canceling a wedding so close to the date is nothing I will ever care to congratulate myself for doing, but I did learn a very difficult lesson: to thine own self be true; even if it's excruciatingly painful.

Johanna McCloy is a writer, editor, and actor. She is the editor of Dare to be Fabulous *as well as her mother's memoir,* Six Car Lengths Behind an Elephant *by Lillian McCloy.*

What's the most emotionally difficult decision you've followed through with in order to remain true to yourself?

"I'm not funny. What I am is brave."

~ Lucille Ball

ALEXANDRA RUSHFIELD

A Comedy Writer's Story

Have you ever wondered what it would be like to be invisible? You probably imagine a scenario like this: you, listening in on your best friend's conversations, find out what everyone really thinks of you. You are happily surprised to discover that while they think you have a big mouth and cannot be trusted with secrets, they consider you loyal and think you've been looking better than ever these days. Okay, slow down. That's not the kind of benign invisibility I'm talking about.

Have you ever sat with eight to ten of the funniest people you've ever met, said something you thought was one of the most hilarious things your brain has ever managed to conjure up, and suddenly felt invisible? Not even like you ceased to exist, more like you never existed in the first place. Pairs of eyes glazing over you as if you were only an empty chair, or worse, looking right through you, as if you were made of air. Invisible.

That is what happened to me in the writers' room. More specifically, the writers' room of a TV comedy show. In 2001, when I just started out working in TV comedy, I worked in one of the most difficult writers' rooms there is, Judd Apatow's, on his show, *Undeclared*. It was difficult in the way you want a writers' room to be difficult — everyone was so good at what they did, it was hard to make a dent. It was like sitting at a dinner table surrounded by sharp wits, all day, every day.

But I couldn't sit there silently and pick at my food. This was my job. I was being paid. I was expected to pull my weight.

The range of reactions to my jokes (and everyone else's) ranged from being invisible to being made fun of mercilessly, so much so, that whatever joke you happened to make became a nickname that could follow you for the rest of your career. (The story isn't worth retelling here, but I was known as "Cranky Pastrami" for a time during *Undeclared*.)

Let me just point out the obvious perks: free food, free Red Vines, free soda and candy, free paper and pens (I haven't paid for a pen in over 15 years.) It is the greatest job in the world. The only downsides are the dangers of invisibility or humiliation, as well as mockery of your age, gender, race, religion, etc. I also want to point out that I have no memory of ever having my feelings hurt in the writers' room over one of my missed attempts at a joke. It was embarrassing on those occasions, maybe, but the environment was never threatening. These people became my best friends.

Eventually, I developed a skin to the humiliation. The moments of being mocked, rejected or just ignored became a positive. It made the skin stronger, until it was an almost armadillo-like shell. Once that skin was there, I could do anything. I could say anything. I was on a suicide mission. Nothing could hurt me.

I contributed my real-life story of flying, which became the air marshal story in the movie *Bridesmaids* (though in my true-life tale, the guy was not actually an air marshal.) I also went to a joke writing session for the movie *Anchorman* and was initially in awe. Will Ferrell. Adam McKay. Steve Carell. It was the most intimidating writers' room I could imagine, but I remembered that I had that skin and that I had built it up for exactly this kind of situation. I don't remember what I said, but I know I made everyone laugh. It was a career high.

For a while I felt invincible in the writers' room. My skin was thick. I could say and do anything without fear of embarrassment or taunting. If anyone tried to mock me, I mocked back (not necessarily my proudest). That skin had reached its maximum strength. It was as if I was a knight or an armadillo. Untouchable.

Then, things changed. I started work on a new show (new for me anyway, it had been on the air for four seasons by that point). The show was *Parks and Recreation*. It's a funny show. I'm a funny writer. I assumed it would be a perfect fit. But *Parks and Rec* was not my finest hour. I couldn't click with the show. I pitched jokes that people thought were funny, but almost never were right for the episode we were working on. I remember throwing something out there for the main character, which I thought was particularly hilarious, and the show runner responded by saying, "That would be amazing . . . if she were out of her fucking mind."

My carefully developed skin was eroding, and it was all because I had become cocky. Now, that skin thinned down to something akin to an old grape. I thought I no longer had feelings when it came to the writers' room. But I did. I realized this because now everything seemed to be hurting my feelings. There was a day when everyone ordered individual chicken potpies for lunch. I was out of the room and they forgot about me, so when the potpies showed up and there wasn't one for me, I actually went into my office and cried. A thick-skinned powerhouse does not cry alone because of a potpie. But I did. My reign was over. Or so I thought. I left the job feeling like I had, for the first time, failed.

Don't worry. This story has a happy ending. I spent two years away from the writers' room and wrote my own stuff. I drew cartoons. One was published in *The New Yorker*. My confidence came back eventually. I created the shows *Shrill* on Hulu and *Santa Inc.* on HBO MAX, both of which gave me new challenges, but ultimately nothing compared to my first years in the writers' room. To date, my skin isn't particularly thick or thin. I'm not cocky, but I feel confident. I have found a middle ground.

Alexandra Rushfield is a TV comedy writer and producer. She was a writer and co-executive producer of Undeclared, Parks and Recreation, Love, *and* Friends from College *and was co- creator and executive producer of* Help Me Help You, In the Motherhood, *and* Shrill, *and was creator and executive producer of* Santa Inc. *She is currently recovering from years of non-stop work and trying to figure out what is next.*

A prompt from Alexandra for TV comedy writers: Write one two-page scene of your show or an already existing comedy, then spend no more than 15 minutes writing as many alternative jokes as possible for the jokes you wrote. Aim for 10 alts for each joke.

"It is the sweet simple things in life which are the real ones after all."

~ Laura Ingalls Wilder

The Fabulosity of Simplicity

I got sober in Alcoholics Anonymous in 1997, following a 20-year drinking run that began with fun, games, ease, debauchery, and adventure . . . and ended up with me as a 33-year-old housewife with a quart-a-day vodka habit.

I was bankrupt in soul, damaged of liver, sluggish, guilty, lying, and dodging. A mom to a darling toddler and wife to a kind, wry, hard-working man. I had become a bit of a shut-in, drinking while my son napped, watched cartoons, and played (often, to my horror, with my ever-present bottles, like sinister toys.) I was in the fortunate position of being able to quit my job in publishing and become a full-time mom. My husband worked long hours as a computer expert at a bank yet still came home to be an attentive, loving dad. But I took this great opportunity and brought it to the precipice of ruin. I was at a desperate impasse and had the fleeting notion that it would take an act outside my own stubborn self to get me the help I needed.

It was my beloved son who ratted me out, blew my cover, and saved my life. My bottles (quarts of 100-proof Smirnoff) were always in my purse, and they went everywhere with me. (I called it my portable bar; a sad "joke" known only to myself.) One day, I got careless with the placement of my bag and — unbeknownst to me — my little son dragged my husband over to my bottle-laden bag. This happened a second time and a third. Then my intuitive baby led my husband to a vodka-soaked shirt I had hastily tossed into the hamper. After that, my husband (quick study that he was) checked quietly for the evidence on his own . . . always, but always, finding it.

He was baffled and horrified by the amount of alcohol I was consuming and devastated by my lying about it. It all came to a heartbreaking showdown that got me into the rooms of Alcoholics Anonymous in 1997, where I gratefully remain to this day. It saved my life, restored my sanity, and slowly rebuilt trust in what today is a happy marriage to the same man. It allowed me to be a gleeful, quirky, loving, responsible mom to my kid, who is now a thriving, independent adult.

But it was a broken, contrite, slightly jaundiced, wounded broad who walked into her first Alcoholics Anonymous meeting. It was in a location known to me; a nearby storefront that was always the site of a cluster of people laughing, chatting, and congregating. I had long figured it to be a 12-Step group of some sort and often thought, "I'll probably have to go there one day, but they haven't gotten me yet!" In time, I called AA for a local meeting place and a sweet, woolly-voiced gentleman provided me with that precise address.

They got me.

It's a tiny room, a cold-water flat that was once a milliner's shop in the 1950s, a gritty Greenwich Village structure if ever there was one. The people inside are like me — struggling with a disease that we cannot combat alone. I attend many meetings all over Manhattan (and all over the globe online during the COVID pandemic), but this one locale has become my spiritual home, my support group, my place to give back, and my connection to the outside world. It has also returned me to my family in better condition than before. And it has allowed me to take my own experience to help others and ensure my ongoing redemption.

My life is, in short, beyond my wildest dreams.

Having shared all that, it's my bemused pleasure to report that a life beyond my wildest dreams turns out to be a mellow, scandal-free existence. It's a safe bet that no one would want to read my sober memoirs. When people share their problems, heartbreaks, and concerns with me and then ask me how I am, I often don't have a whole lot to report.

I do some volunteer work, lots of service within the 12-step rooms, design jewelry on a whim, and acquired a wonderful freelance writing gig for a website that celebrates vintage pop culture. My husband is a fairly young retiree, very immersed in the community, and we're gratifyingly comfortable in the city of my dreams.

My life is filled with small joys, each set off with the daily conscious awareness that I am upright, healthy, sane, and happy . . . entirely as a result of my day-at-a-time sobriety.

I have reams of books, love watching crime TV shows and old movies, live in Greenwich Village (not the Bohemian Nirvana I fell in love with, alas, but a trove of delights nonetheless) and stay within a pretty tight 10-block radius for the most part. I'm endlessly immersed in music. I hoof it everywhere, greet my doormen (and the next building's doormen) like the old friends they are, love the deli guys, shoot the breeze with familiar faces on the street, hide out when I see fit. I have a bunch of go-to tea stores, hippie shops, diners, and pizzerias that become homes away from home.

When I was younger, I'm sure I expected a little more glitz, bang for my buck, funky talking points in my existence, but that's not quite what happened. I don't come with a series of exciting anecdotes, but I'm treated with kindness and respect, looked to for advice and comfort. Astoundingly, I connect with people in ways I would have found impossible when I was busily hiding out in the bottle.

Life's not perfect, nor need it be. I've had my share of disappointments, losses of loved ones, broken bones, health scares, friendship weirdness, and agita during the past 24 years, make no mistake. It's just life, on life's terms. But the endless upside is that I am present and accountable to all of it, get to amend the wrongs, make fewer of them, not destroy myself on a daily basis, and even give back to my world a little bit.

It's a modest, fulfilling existence. I wouldn't trade it for anything. I work hard to maintain it, but the benefits are peace, ease, a certain comfort in my skin, and bursts of quiet, profound gratitude. I'm not only above ground, I'm (metaphorically, mind you) dancing in the aisles.

Alcoholic Anonymous is a 58-year-old sober wife, mom, citizen, happy left-wing broad, voracious reader, lover of all things vintage & long-time resident of Greenwich Village.

Alcoholic Anonymous writes about her AA meeting: "the people inside are like me — struggling with a disease that we cannot combat alone." Have you ever attended a support group meeting, or considered doing so? Write about why it's helpful to be in the company of "strangers" who understand. If you've considered attending a support group meeting, take this opportunity to locate one near you.

"Follow your passion. Stay true to yourself. Never follow someone else's path unless you're in the woods and you're lost and you see a path. By all means, you should follow that."

~ Ellen DeGeneres

Sola Peddling

During the summer after I graduated from high school, I made a new friend in the neighborhood. We did heaps of outdoorsy things together and soon began planning a bike-riding trip through the Mediterranean. He preferred the idea of a boys' beer adventure trip with his brother, so I decided that biking around Europe alone would suit me fine. I had been an exchange student in Venezuela and had done a fair amount of traveling with my family. I was craving independence and anonymity.

I decided to visit Corsica, Sardinia, Italy, and the Greek Islands. I agreed to call home once a week. (Internet and cell phones were things of the future.) I was only 17 and didn't have a credit card, so I planned diligent use of my traveler's checks. I would pack lightly and stay in youth hostels along my route. I would rely on my high school French and some perfunctory Greek that lay dormant from having lived there as a small child. I had no experience speaking Italian, but seeing the beautiful Italian countryside was a top priority. I would muddle through any language deficiencies.

I landed in Pisa and after a bit of greasy bike finagling, I was soon happily pedaling. All went well during those early days in the countryside. I enjoyed meandering and carefully composing photos I wouldn't see until later, when I had the film developed. Youth hostel life was mostly straightforward. I slept in my own 'sheet sleeping bag' that

I had sewn, which helped give me a familiar feeling every night, and I ate well from the fruit stalls, delis, and bakeries in every town. Lots of pointing on my part and eyebrow raising by those behind the counters was the norm as I attempted Italian phrasing about all things delicious.

I was strategic in planning my daily rides, because a miscalculation could find me cycling in the dark. With the same logic that had me omit a bike repair kit, I had reasoned that I didn't need lights, since I didn't plan to use them. Now, looking back at that trip from the perspective of a middle-aged mother of three who doesn't leave the house without an armament of provisions and clothing, I find the mindset of my teenaged-self baffling.

I blissfully soaked up every detail of the bucolic scenery on the quiet back roads, enjoying the rhythmic pace of contemplative pedaling. The friendly people I passed were curious and spoke to me. I saw them watering their yards, playing with their children and grandchildren, walking their dogs, and pegging laundry. Seeing me alone bolstered their courage to engage me and their eyes widened with incredulity when I answered their questions:

"*Sí, Canadese.*"

"*Sí, sono sola*"

"*Corsica, Sardinia e Grecia il prossimi.*"

Their surprised reactions turned into amusement when I offered a confident smile. Many gave me a variation of the "Go for it!" sign.

I explored Italy and Corsica before I took a ship to Sardinia. I was keen to see the island's lush pastoral areas, quaint country towns, and "Emerald Coast" beaches. As I straddled my bright yellow bike and surveyed the landscape from a vantage spot on the ship's upper deck, I realized that I had neglected one crucial element of geographical research: topography. Sardinia is a small island, but flat it is not. As I quickly recalculated the distances on my map, I feared I wouldn't make it to the hostel before it got dark. Increasing my pace was my only option, so I pedaled with fervor up hills and down valleys, through craggy green terrain crisscrossed with rock walls that only vaguely restrained intrepid sheep. When I finally arrived at the hostel location, I found only an empty lot.

Exhausted and confused, I coasted down the main street of the quiet coastal town just as the sun was setting. I asked a shop-owner who was closing up for directions. I pointed at the little red house icon on the map that denoted the hostel. He removed his glasses to take a closer look and came up bleak-faced. He said something to his young son who was standing at his side, and then his son said in English, "Hotel, no. Next year to build." I thanked them and had little choice but to check into a tiny *pensione* at the end of the street where I enjoyed a night of luxury. I had a bath in a private ensuite and then climbed under the freshly laundered sheets of a comfortable bed.

The sleep was transformative and I spent the next day exploring the town, swimming at the beach, and admiring all the yachts in the marina. I got into a pleasant conversation (in English, hurrah!) with a couple of sailors who invited me to join them on their sailing adventures to Greece. Both men were probably only in their 30s, but looked older, their heavily tanned faces already deeply lined. Fear of being alone with men I didn't know caused me to decline, but looking back, I think I missed that they were likely a romantically involved couple just wanting to offer safe passage to a pint-sized female teen traveling alone.

I continued south where the turquoise beaches were long and shimmered like countless dancing fairies. I spent a couple nights glamping and passed unhurried days lounging on the beach trying to read the local paper. When it was time to retrace my path, I decided instead to avoid the Sardinian Rockies and take the train. In order to make the train to catch the boat I had to leave at 3:00 a.m. The moon lit my path like a giant bulb in an otherwise inky sky. The gravel road before me was busy with critters, furry and otherwise, crossing to and fro. I heard crickets and the sounds of birds stirring in the cool morning air as I searched for courage in the pre-dawn light. I settled into a rhythm but faltered when a pair of headlights appeared over a rise. Panicking that I could be abducted by some ne'er-do-well Sardinian, (who else but a deranged person would be driving a lonely road at this ungodly hour?), I quickly ran my bike off the road and hid in the ditch, holding my breath until I saw it was just a pickup truck filled with crates of produce. It rumbled past sedately.

As the sun crept up the horizon, I found breakfast at an already bustling bakery and ate on a bench outside the train station. When I loaded my bike into the passenger compartment of the train, I was surprised to see the car was made almost entirely of wood and was open to the sky and had heavy fabric above like a ragtop convertible. A handsome gentleman entered the car at the first stop and eyed me curiously. He was middle-aged and elegantly dressed in a linen suit. He checked his pocket watch when the train abruptly stopped and sat idle on the track for a few minutes. I leaned out the side of the rickety trolley, but all I could see were rows of densely leafed trees. The gentleman offered a quick burst of Italian by way of explanation, but I was no closer to understanding the level of our predicament. How bad could it be? Likely it was sheep on the track or maybe it was a stalled delivery van full of pastries, or gelato at risk of melting?! My musings over delays of possible yumminess were interrupted when the train conductor suddenly appeared in our compartment, looking pink-faced and warm in his thick sweater and cap, carrying a basket full of cherries.

"A stop to pick cherries?" I thought. "Italy!! You do not disappoint!"

He gestured for us to share the bounty and moments later we were on our way. The be-suited gentleman and I each took a large handful and passed the basket back. The cherries were small but incredibly sweet and we munched in tasty silence, throwing pits out the side of the train car until the gentleman worked up the courage to ask me the usual questions.

"Canada?! *Eppa!*" he said with an expansive arm gesture and gold-toothed smile. The fact I was alone AND traveling by bicycle seemed beyond his comprehension. He pulled out his wallet and I had a moment of confusion until he carefully eased out a couple of photos and began pointing animatedly. I managed to understand that he was on his way to his son's 20th birthday party. His wife and whole family were already there, cooking. There would be music and dancing and the most delicious "*torta al limone*" at the party and would I please attend? The photo of his son revealed him to be very handsome and his father gave me a knowing nod. He complimented my physique (miming, 'strong' and 'pretty') and said something about "*bambini Canadesi*" and pointed to my blue eyes and winked mischievously.

Even though we had shared food and pleasant, albeit mostly-mimed, conversation I didn't feel inclined to abandon my plans as his stop approached. I lamented my poor language skills hadn't allowed me to fully explain that I had to have already planned where I would stay the upcoming night. But I suspected it was better that way because I felt sure he would have offered me a bed for the night, and I was almost as sure his son might have been in it! So, I missed singing "*Buon Compleanno*" and carried on to meet my boat bound for Greece.

In Greece, I transited quickly out to the islands and settled on Santorini. There, I stayed in their derelict but oh-so-much fun hostel for a week. I met a crazy Canadian girl who got me into no end of adventures including topless sun tanning, late night dancing, and ouzo. (My bicycle didn't move.)

At the end of my trip, as I waited for the plane to take off from Athens, I breathed a satisfied sigh. It had been a risky undertaking, to say the least, navigating alone with neither credit card nor phone, but I managed it. I had enjoyed myself and learned enormously. I've read that growth occurs in the space outside one's comfort zone. I'm not sure why I had to go to the other side of the world to leave my small comfort zone, but that's when I learned to listen to my own voice. (Maybe that's partly because it was one of the few I heard in English?)

Today, most of my adventures are less about far-flung locales and more about far-flung soccer socks. As a full-time parent I have graduated from the tasks of potty training and supervising play dates to the realm of helping to guide appropriate screen use and class selections. I encourage our children to listen to their own voices, and I wonder which paths they will choose to take. Our eldest is nearing the age I was when I first ventured out. I know the worry I will feel when she tells me she wants to do something alone, but I also know that my "*sola*" pedaling gave me much of the confidence and resourcefulness that is the foundation of my life today.

Carter Helliwell is an artist and writer who lives on an island on Western Canada's most southerly tip. Her blog chronicles her life's sometimes rocky but mostly happily enlightening journeys from far and near.

Imagine a solo trip of your own. As a teenager right out of high school or as the person you are right now. Where would you go? What would you do?

"If we're going to find our way out of shame
and back to each other, vulnerability is
the path and courage is the light . . .
To love ourselves and support each other
in the process of becoming real is perhaps
the greatest single act of daring greatly."

~ Brené Brown

MOINA SHAIQ

Meet a Muslim

I have been involved in interfaith work for over a decade and the same open-minded and receptive people attend our events, so it often feels like we're preaching to the choir. Not that this is bad; in fact, it builds stronger relationships and deeper understanding amongst those who already know about Islam and the Muslim way of life. Still, I want to reach out to people who are not coming to these interfaith events. I want to talk to people who have never met a Muslim.

Research indicates that 80% of Americans have never met a Muslim. Most people will identify Muslims as a woman wearing a headscarf (*hijab*) or a man with a beard and a turban. The fact is that only 20% of Muslim women wear a hijab and almost no Muslim man wears a turban.

9/11 changed my life. In the aftermath of this crisis, I stayed home for 10 days. My family was very scared of a backlash, and since I wear the hijab, they didn't let me go out. I knew that many people were uninformed about Islam and that their lack of knowledge or personal exposure to Muslims was prompting fear. I decided that I wanted my fellow Americans to know about my faith, so I started getting involved in the community, attending as many city events as possible, showing my face everywhere.

On the day after the 2009 Fort Hood shooting (when a radicalized "Muslim" Marine opened fire and killed several of his colleagues), I dropped my daughter off at soccer practice. Usually, after dropping her off, I would walk around the park, but that day I couldn't bring myself to do it. I was feeling guilty, like I had done something wrong. Beyond that, I was truly scared. After sitting in my car for a while, I thought, I can't just sit here. Somehow, I drummed up the courage and got out of my car. I walked, but I couldn't make eye contact with anyone. I felt as if I had done something wrong. When I posted this on Facebook, a Christian friend was so moved that she wore a hijab the next day, not only to commute to work, but the whole day, in solidarity.

After the 2015 Paris and San Bernardino shootings (perpetrated by radicalized individuals who called themselves Muslims), I decided to place an ad titled "Meet a Muslim" in the local paper. My plan was to spend an hour at a local coffee shop. I thought that if someone came, I could talk to them, and if not, I would just continue working on my laptop so as not to waste time.

A non-Muslim friend noticed my "Meet a Muslim" ad and called to relay his concern about my safety. He said that by putting myself out there, I could become a very easy target. He encouraged me to contact the police and inform them of my plans. So, I did. I informed the police chief and he immediately offered to send an officer to the event.

I thought a few people might come, but over a 100 people attended the event. There was no place to sit for the attendees and it was overwhelming. I invited people to ask me anything; no question would be off-limits. They had all sorts of questions, mostly related to current events. Questions like, Why are women oppressed in Islam? What is Sharia Law? What is the difference between Shia and Sunni? What is terrorism and why are Muslims getting radicalized? They didn't ask me any personal questions.

I really wanted to share my personal story and to relay that I am an ordinary American, just like they are. I am someone they might see at their local grocery store, at the mall, or on the street. I am a mother, a wife, and a daughter, and I have been a community member for 40 years. I have four beautiful children. One was born in North Carolina, the second one in Texas, and my last two in Fremont, California, where I live. All my kids went through Fremont schools.

I have been a Little League, football, and soccer mom. My son is also an Eagle Scout and I am very proud of him. My husband and I have purchased our burial plots here in Fremont, and we intend to die here.

In addition to my mom-related activities, I have served as a Human Relations Commissioner for the city of Fremont, served on County Commissions, and joined the boards of several non-profit organizations, because I am passionate about their work. In the process, of course, they've learned about me too.

I have hosted over 150 "Meet a Muslim" events as of this writing, and thank God, most people have been very respectful. There was one event when a guy said that he would cut my throat if I offended him. He also said that he was armed with a knife. At first, I was speechless. I could not imagine why a fellow American would say something as intense as this. However, I then became thankful to him for finding the courage to come. After all, these are the people who are ignorant and who we need to reach out to. I want to build bridges of love, understanding, and acceptance.

One beautiful aspect of these events is the way my friends from different faiths have participated. My technology guru is a very close Jewish friend who does social media for a living, but she helps me behind the scenes, because she is very supportive of my cause and wants to bring the community together. Another friend is a Deacon at a local church, and he has come to all of my events. When he thinks that an answer to a particular question might be better understood if people also hear his perspective, he'll offer that input. For example, when I've been asked about Sharia law, he will offer an analogy to Canon laws in Christianity, or Halakha laws in Judaism to help further explain. Moreover, another Christian friend went with me to Arizona when I hosted events there. She, too, was concerned about my safety.

In my "Meet a Muslim" events, I share the five pillars of Islam in order to give the audience a basic understanding of my faith. I tell them that human beings have shed a lot of blood throughout history in the name of religion, but that no religion condones such acts. It is we who misconstrue verses, take them out of context, and act upon them. When that happens, it is generally about wanting control and power.

I also emphasize that no one is born with a symbol on his or her body, like a cross or a Star of David. No two people are alike, unless they are identical twins, and even they have different personalities. Two sisters raised in the same family are different. How can we expect people from a different faith to all be the same? Of course, people may look different, have a different culture, and eat different foods, but at the end of the day, we all have the same basic needs of food and shelter. We all want the best for our children and want to live our lives in peace and harmony.

In the Muslim faith, we are to love our neighbors. In this spirit, I want to reach out to as many people as I can. I have spoken at places of worship, service group meetings, schools, colleges, coffee shops, senior living facilities, a mobile home park, a pizza place, and people's homes. At the end of each event, audience members ask me, "What can we do now?" I tell them to work as ambassadors. They need to help their family members, friends, co-workers, or neighbors understand Islam and Muslims. I'd love to see those conversations happening in every community in the United States.

My "Meet a Muslim" conversations have received a lot of media coverage, including a cover story in *The San Francisco Chronicle* and features in television news programs, including CNN. My story also appeared in the *Christian Science Monitor*.

I have a dedicated "Meet a Muslim" Facebook page for people to get more information. I hope you'll join me there.

And yes, I do speak Urdu.

Moina Shaiq has been living in the United States for 43 years. She is a mother of four children and a grandmother of six. She has a Bachelor's Degree in Psychology and Economics. She is also a community activist, devoting herself to building bridges of understanding.

A prompt from Moina: Humanity is not a singular culture. Let's learn about each other and help make this world a more compassionate place.

Think about an experience in your life that helped you become more open, understanding, and compassionate toward a previously unfamiliar group of people (based on religion, culture, language, sexual preference, gender, or ethnicity). Did you overcome an initial sense of judgment or fear? How did your perspective shift?

"I look forward to growing old
and wise and audacious."

~ Glenda Jackson

MICHELE MAGGIORA

Ode to Gray

I wanted to stop but I kept at it; the ritual of dyeing my hair. I had colored my hair since my twenties, long before I started to gray. I used cellophane rinses and colors of eggplant, red, and burgundy until those telltale hairs began to show. Then I began to wash that gray away and continued until my fifty-eighth year.

This monthly ritual escalated into a bi-monthly project in later years to hide the silvering roots that glared from the crown of my head, never realizing what I was, almost blindly, trying to preserve. I did not associate my action with the underlying fear of losing my power by losing my youthful beauty.

My older sister never dyed her hair. Although we often shared the same soapbox on women's issues, I kept dyeing. When she questioned my continued coverage of the blossoming of my gray, I had a litany of defenses: our grandmother grayed young and I'm not ready to look like grandma, my skin wouldn't look right with gray hair, and I'm dramatic and love changing my look as a raven-wing beauty! I admired my sister's wild salt-and-pepper hair, but it wasn't for me. I convinced myself of my choice without regard for the underlying reasons lurking in my psyche.

And besides, everyone does it.

My husband at the time was completely gray.

"Don't dye your hair for me," he kept saying.

"I'm almost ready to go natural," I assured him, only to greet him later with the same reddish-brown hair. My husband was Mr. Natural; my continuance of masking what was becoming natural annoyed him.

Although there was no mistaking the reality — my hair was a faded red tone, more brittle and generally less lustrous, but my stomach tightened.

"I can do what I want to do, it's my hair!" I screeched.

"I'm tired of trying to please everyone!"

I burst into tears.

"The truth is I'm afraid! I'm afraid of losing something and getting old!"

In that final honest moment, a tiny ray of light was shed on what I had refused to see — *that doing what I wanted* was more attached to survival programming than to my authentic self. Throughout the ages and exacerbated in the modern world, many cultures held powerful deep-seated beliefs about women and aging.

I found relief in the exquisite photos of Native American women: faces that expressed beauty, intuition, and power. They were the gray-haired elders and wise women whose faces, carved deeply with lines and surrounded by gray, proudly expressed their lives. They had achieved wise woman status. I realized that the key to their pride and elder beauty rested in the respect and honor of their position.

In my fifties, while living in Oaxaca, Mexico, I worked with indigenous Zapotec women from Salina Cruz. Graying naturally, the women tied their hair into long braids woven with strips of brightly colored cloth — luminous faces, luminous gray hair. The movement into elderhood was honored. These gray-haired elders held the heart of the community both spiritually and politically. Non-indigenous *Mexicanas*, following the modern Western paradigm, continued dyeing and were as raven-haired as I.

Later, recalling images of my mother, a beautiful and creative woman, I understood how it was seriously important for her to give me *tools* for survival as a woman. Once, after expressing resentment about the annoying invasion from construction workers with their hoots and whistles, my mother quipped, "You'd better start worrying when they stop whistling!" Other such *tools* included her suggestion to fake orgasm to protect the frail male ego and her consistent evaluation of my hair, make-up, and figure.

I have forgiven my mother because she was giving me the same tools she was given: the legacy of female survival as it is passed through the ages from mother to daughter. The intention of this survival training was not to stifle the spirit (although it did) but to help one survive in a male-dominant culture. This insistence of this legacy clearly demonstrates the narrow ground of power afforded to women.

Historically, women have been taught that access to power comes through their connection to those who hold it: men. There are changes today. Women have access to more positions in the world, although defined predominantly in male terms. The need to be validated by a man (heterosexual) continues. When we carve away parts of our spirit and authentic selves in order to be validated, we perpetuate the ancestral legacy.

Or we can unravel this constricted cultural reality, see the illusion, and muster the courage to embrace our freedom.

I vividly remember the exact pivot point. I was visiting my sister, telling her of my intention to mentor younger women.

"So, you are going to mentor younger women? How can you do it with that hair!"

My sister went for it. I looked in the mirror and saw the faded red-brown hair; hair I always disliked on older women. I was that woman. I was trying to prop up an illusion and was losing the battle. I looked harsh and faded. I saw fear in my eyes.

When I got home, I called my hair stylist, Carlos. He gave me an appointment immediately. Carlos began to strip the color from my faded red hair. "Michele, it's not about looking young, it's about looking good," he said. And now after some months, I know it's not only about looking good. It's about embracing our *medicine*, the Medicine of the Elder, the wise woman bursting with beauty!

So how do I do this? I was willing to become aware, to be uncomfortable, and face my fears. I looked at cultural attitudes and how we raise our daughters. I listened to how I felt about myself and noted how those feelings came from programmed thoughts. I knew then that I had to be ruthlessly honest and courageous, even if I was shaking in my boots. I began to redefine age, beauty, power, value, and what brings self-love.

This is never an easy journey, because we live in a modern culture where the collective unconscious underpinnings constantly reinforce our fear of getting old and worthless. I realize why I love the old faces of Native women . . . because they are truly beautiful! These are faces filled with personal power. They respect themselves as they are honored by their people. Getting old holds no disgrace. On the contrary, it is an honored era in a woman's life, a time of wisdom, beauty, authenticity, and personal power.

I believe we have a duty, an obligation to shift the legacy and to take ownership of our beauty, our wisdom, our relevance, and our substance. By doing so, we open the possibilities of a new reality for ourselves, our daughters, all women, and all humanity.

Michele Maggiora stopped dyeing her hair shortly before turning 59 years old. "My writings often point to the political and social connections between sexism, racism, and classism." She currently lives in Mexico and works as a mentor, writer, visual artist, poet, and photographer.

What conventional or cultural beauty standards have you defied, or plan to defy, in order to feel more authentically YOU?

"She found joy and wonder in every little thing. And joy and wonder always found her."

~ Katrina Mayer

ANNA ELKINS

"We Can Read!"

"I can read. I can tie my shoes. I have food in the fridge." These are the kinds of things my down-the-street neighbor tells herself when she's feeling off or blue — basic, often overlooked things worth giving thanks for.

The other day, I met my *up-the-street* neighbor. We talked about life, relationships, and the pain and joy in both. We were trying to focus on the good stuff and not worry about the bad stuff. As I was leaving, I remembered my other neighbor and her gratitude. I said, "I think gratitude is the anecdote to anxiety. Wait . . . I mean antidote. Wait . . . I mean both!"

And there on her doorstep, I had a revelation. When we tell our stories of gratitude — the anecdotes — we create the antidote to the bad stuff: fear, anxiety, annoyance, and all the nasty etceteras.

I can testify: it works.

Try it yourself: Think of something un-good that you felt recently. Feel that feeling. Here's (one of) mine: annoyance. I was walking in the Woodlands where people ignore the signs requiring dogs to be on leashes. A dog bounded toward me, leash-less. His owner yelled out, "Don't worry, he's friendly." Yeah, well, friendly means he's jumping up on my bare calves after having run off-trail through the poison oak. I wanted to yell out, "Can't you read the signs? Can't you take responsibility for your actions?" And in my head, the scenario spun

121

into global proportions where all people were hopeless and I was a fuming misanthropist.

Stop.

Now, start listing things you're grateful for — anything on the spectrum.

I give thanks for my nose.

I give thanks for the fact that I can walk.

I give thanks for the Woodlands someone bequeathed to this town.

I give thanks for trees that give shade, provide homes for birds, and clean the air that I am able to breathe through my nose as I walk in these woods....

I created an anecdote of gratitude that became an antidote to the nasty. Notice that it started with the thing literally in front of me: my nose. The more annoyed I am, the more basic the beginning, but those details inevitably build into a story of gratitude. I also moved from the little problem by reminding myself of the bigger narrative of life. I used a silly example to keep it light, but believe me: I've tried it on the Big Bads too. It still works.

Sometimes I begin with "I am grateful for . . ." or "Thank you for . . .," but I have come to like "I give thanks for . . ." the best. It makes me an active "thanker." It tells my inner pouty self: "You are choosing this good thing over this bad one. No matter what the bad thing is, you can still choose your attitude about it."

When I practice this gratitude exercise, the annoyance dissolves. I discovered something I'm sure someone else has already discovered: that you can't be grateful and annoyed (or angry, or anxious) at the same time. You have to let one of them go.

Now, dog paws in the woods are one thing. You might ask: what about divorce? Death? War? I'm not saying that if you drop and give 20 "thank-yous" in the midst of a military campaign that we'll immediately have world peace. But then again . . . what if everybody did? What if everyone tried trading in their hurt, pain, and anger for gratitude? What might happen?

I'm grateful for grace, too — even (especially) toward myself. Just this morning, I indulged in frustration as a momentarily spotty internet connection delayed some research for another essay. So, I gave thanks for my neighbors — those two friends whose anecdotes have become part of my antidote. And then I was in it again: the story of gratitude.

I choose to give thanks, thank you very much.

Anna Elkins is a poet and painter. She earned a B.A. in art and English and an M.F.A. and Fulbright Fellowship in poetry. Her poetry collection Hope of Stones *won the 2021 Oregon Book Award. Anna has written, painted, and taught on six continents and now lives in a tiny town near the Rogue River with her husband.*

A prompt from Anna: Gratitude is powerful — both in life and in writing. Create a list of 10 things you're grateful for, beginning each line with "I give thanks for . . ." Vary your list: use a mix of single words, phrases, and full paragraphs. See how one item might inspire the next. Feeling inspired? List ten more. See where gratitude takes you.

"People said, 'Jane, forget about this nonsense with Africa. Dream about things you can achieve.'"

~ Jane Goodall

JILL ROBINSON, MBE

Her Name Was Hong

Destiny. A word that conjures a world of hope and change — a word that makes us shiver after our lives have been shifted and redirected forever by a fateful moment in time. Accepting it, embracing it, and knowing instinctively that there is no going back. At 35 years of age, leaving my home in Hong Kong for a day trip to mainland China, the gentle hand of destiny took mine, and everything changed . . . everything changed.

Her name was Hong — at least that was the name I gave to the first bear I ever saw in one of Asia's notorious "bile extraction" farms.

It was April 1993. I was working for the International Fund for Animal Welfare, and took a call from a journalist friend who urged me to visit a bear bile farm in China from which he'd just returned.

I was intrigued and nervous, having never visited such a place before, and knowing nothing about the species of Asiatic black bears (or moon bears, so described after the glorious crescent moon of lemony fur on their chests), nor about the bear bile farming industry itself.

About a week later, I joined a group of tourists and entered the farm in southern China, where the farmer and his wife were boasting outside the entrance of their shop about everything their bile could cure. There was a circular "bear pit" of breeding bears nearby and the farmer was encouraging tourists to buy apples on strings with which to tease them. The bears, made to stand bipedally on their back

125

legs, were teased with fruit dangling inches away from their hungry mouths, while the tourists all laughed.

As many people bought the apples or bile products from the shop, I took the opportunity to sneak away and find the victims of bile extraction, and found a doorway leading to a basement where the caged bears were kept.

Absolutely nothing prepared me for that moment. Thirty-two moon bears blinked forlornly out of their "crush cages" and made nervous popping vocalizations every time I approached them — clearly anticipating something terrible was going to happen. As I looked more closely, I saw why they were afraid. Years of cage confinement saw scars running three or four feet in length along their bodies, teeth smashed from repetitive and frustrated bar biting, others with teeth and paw tips deliberately cut away to make them less dangerous to handle and, worst of all, long metal catheters poking out from infected holes in their abdomens, from which they extracted their bile for use in traditional medicine.

Never had I felt more shocked or helpless, sick to my stomach with the reality of what these creatures had suffered over decades of being exploited for a body fluid that could so easily be replaced with herbs or synthetics. Suddenly I felt something touch my shoulder, and turned around in shock to see a female moon bear reaching her paw through the cage. At that moment, it seemed simply right to take her mighty paw in my hand and, rather than hurting me as I know now that she could have done, she squeezed my fingers, held my eyes with hers, and the message was clear.

I knew instinctively that I would never see her again — but my message back to her was equally clear. She would become the ambassador for my promise that bear farming would one day end. I named her Hong, which means bear in Cantonese, and though I feel overwhelming sorrow at knowing that I couldn't save her, Hong is responsible for every step I've taken since.

I founded Animals Asia in 1998, and constructed sanctuaries in Chengdu and Vietnam after that. To date, we've rescued over 650 farmed and caged bears, in addition to rescuing and helping other animals all over Asia.

These years have seen significant progress. In 2017, Animals Asia signed a groundbreaking Memorandum of Understanding with the government of Vietnam to end bear bile farming once and for all. The construction of our second sanctuary in Vietnam will now assist the authorities in closing the remaining farms and helping the remaining approximately 400 bears.

Many people may be surprised to know that bear bile works. Despite my naïve conviction in the early days that this was a "quack" medicine, the reality is that bear bile contains an effective bile acid called ursodeoxycholic acid (UDCA) — that is now also synthesized and sold the world over — but not from bears. In truth, it all boils down to the "stakeholders" in the trade and those who profit from an industry.

Another hurdle, inevitably is financial. I have sleepless nights acknowledging that while our sanctuaries are celebrated for both rescuing bears and giving them world-class care and management to the end of their days, our duty of care for their 30-year lifespan is up against such challenging odds.

For there can be no more proud or joyous feeling than to close another farm, break open another cage, and look into an animals' eyes, knowing that you have made a difference, rather than turning away, ashamed, at each new vision of despair. Victims who arrived understandably aggressive and consumed with pain and fear are, today, showing how stoic, trusting, and truly forgiving this species can be.

One of those victims was Jasper.

Jasper was a bear for whom I'd coined the phrase — "as we rescue them, they rescue us." It was Jasper I'd run to when times got tough — Jasper who would calm the most stressful situations, simply by licking peanut butter from the spoon with his soft pink tongue. I would spend hours sitting outside his enclosure as I grappled with the latest problems that were presenting themselves to the team and me. He gave me solace and I looked forward to those quiet meetings with my colleague with the beautiful yellow crescent of fur on his chest and ridiculous Mickey Mouse ears.

How Jasper could be quite so forgiving was always a mystery to me. Caged and crushed flat to the bars on arrival at the sanctuary, with a metal catheter painfully sticking out of his abdomen from where his bile dripped. And yet, from the moment he arrived, he become the "peacemaker" of the sanctuary, showing the indomitable spirit of what must be one of the most forgiving species on the planet.

Supporters and celebrities alike loved meeting Jasper — and he loved meeting new friends, too. Stories are legendary of camera crews going to the bear houses for some "general" bear pictures, and returning to the office asking about the bear with yellow eyebrows, who had gleefully photo-bombed all their shots. Two books have been written about this extraordinary bear, and many stories and films feature him too. Even on the Saturday before he died, he delighted visitors at our Open Day as he rolled around in the grass with his friends.

And that day he said goodbye remains carved in my heart.

"Jill, I'm sorry . . .". With those words from our vet, Eddie, who had tears running down her face as she spoke through her mask, my world came crashing down. Eddie's words took some seconds to sink in. Please, not Jasper . . . not the bear who'd arrived 15 years before in that crude "crush cage" with his mutilated abdomen a mass of infection, and yellow-brown bile dripping onto the floor. Not the bear who, like Hong, even while he suffered, had pushed his paw out of the cage and patted my hand.

But now here he was, lying on the operating table, looking small and vulnerable as Eddie opened him up for exploratory surgery, to check some concerning images that the ultrasound had found. To the shock of all in the room, there was nothing small and vulnerable about the tumor that had taken over the entire central lobe of his liver. Large and aggressive, with a life of its own, it had grown to this proportion in just three short months.

With the news quietly sinking in, it seemed impossible to believe that until that point, Jasper had been behaving pretty much like a healthy, normal bear. I'd smiled the day before to see him sunbathing on the platform in his beloved enclosure. Together with Bear and Vet Team Director Nic, we had fed him dried kiwi, pineapple, and dates, laughing when he looked at some banana in disdain and ignored it, as he always, always did.

Our goodbye to Jasper was inevitable and sad. My tears didn't stop falling, remembering this iconic, forgiving bear who had given our staff and supporters across the world such inspiration and joy.

Today, while regretting we couldn't save Hong, I take comfort in knowing that Jasper had the best and happiest life. I don't think I ever looked at him without laughing out loud, and miss him, achingly so, but am so grateful to him too for the years of love and friendship and for the joy he brought into our lives.

In Jasper's memory, I ask that everyone reading this give a bear hug in celebration of kindness. After all, our unkindness towards animals has led to virtually every pandemic in the world. Hug your family, your friends, your colleagues, your teachers, your cats and your dogs, and even those you wouldn't normally hug too . . . because more than anything our bear hug expert, our peacemaker, our Jasper, would have loved this gesture, as he hugged for China, and embraced his own love of life and kindness with his friends.

Jill Robinson is the founder of Animals Asia, devoted to ending the practice of bear bile farming and improving the welfare of animals in China and Vietnam. Through her work with the bears, and her many other programs administered through Animals Asia, she is at the forefront of changing the way animals are perceived and treated on that continent. In 1998, she was awarded an MBE by Queen Elizabeth in recognition of her services to animal welfare in Asia. In 2002, she received the Genesis Award in the United States — the only major media and arts award concerning animal issues.

The last paragraph of Jill's story serves as a beautiful prompt: "In Jasper's memory, I ask that everyone reading this give a bear hug in celebration of kindness." Read that full paragraph again. Give those generous bear hugs! And please consider giving a virtual bear hug to Jill in the form of whatever donation you can offer to Animals Asia.

"Life is about not knowing, having to change, taking the moment and making the best of it, without knowing what's going to happen next. Delicious ambiguity."

~ Gilda Radner

How Does a Flower Dare to Bloom?

How does a flower dare to bloom a million times over in a million strange places to a million different faces? And how is it that I see you and me, abloom in every new face on the street? How is it possible I'm here at this moment, a whirling manifestation of choices I've made long ago and far away, and choices I've made this very day? This is the face of who I am. The heart burgeoning red with desire and fire. The heart bloody with rhythm and beats. The heart, my heart, shared with affection to closed ears, to countless fears. My heart and my rhythm. And yes, I've been to crossroads where I was pitted fiercely against the me of who I was and the me who I knew I was supposed to be, two opposites and the opportunity to make a choice.

Allow me to share a simple story of one of those moments of crossroads divine. A day I surrendered upon a lake.

It was a hot summer day, a vacation day spent with one of my best friends. We were to commune with nature in the woods of Montana for four glorious days, a much-needed respite from the smog and noise of Los Angeles. However, the trip, as most, was not what we expected, and we were forced to live in a new understanding of what godliness, peace, and nature meant to us. There were challenges every day, and it most certainly was not the laid-back, easy stroll through the forest, soaking in the all-glorious divine weekend we expected.

On one of those days, we hiked to the lake near where we were camping. My spirit was a little down and I, still hoping to gather some much-needed inspiration and guidance from the saturation of nature, was feeling low that life hadn't already jumped out at me and sung to me all the answers I was so desperately seeking. Along the walk, we were trying to be in good spirits, my friend, our Montana guide, and my pitiful, dreary self.

I was feeling insecure because a week later I was going to be seeing a guy whom I hadn't seen in months and whom I dug intensely, but wasn't too sure how he felt about me. My mind was already fully occupied with scenes of impending disaster, all egged on by premenstrual insecurities and quickly turning into monstrous negative thoughts. The part of me inside who was still hopeful of some drastic change of mood was looking forward to the lake, but when we finally got there, we soon discovered mosquitoes and a less than idyllic surrounding. I mean, it was beautiful, just not pleasant.

My friend wasn't going to let that get her down. She stripped down and jumped into the lake before I could lather on repellent. She seemed so free, yet I could not get past the muckiness and the bugs. I was getting deeper and deeper into a funk. I stood there, wanting so badly to just jump in the lake. What was wrong with me? Why was I frozen with inaction?

I was turning into a black hole of doubt and fear. Nothing felt right. I felt so out of place. My friend finally surfaced. We talked for a bit, but decided to head back when the mosquitoes started getting worse. I had missed my chance.

As we began to put our layers back on, I felt like crying. What was I scared of? Maybe I'd be sucked under by some dark demon of my own making and drown? What if some weird flesh-eating fish was in there, just waiting to gnaw on something? It was useless, there was no release from this tangled mood. The three of us started to walk away. Then it hit me; it was the tiniest whisper somewhere in that frozen tundra of fear, a deep knowing that I had to jump in the lake *now*, no turning back.

Without hesitation, I quickly threw off my clothes and dove into the water, far beyond the murky edges. I came up engulfed in sunshine and the cool peace of the lake and I floated there for a while, feeling no more agitation, no more worry, just a oneness with myself, with my own inner knowing, my own breath of life. When I felt my head return to daily thoughts, I swam back to the edge, renewed. My friend, with a knowing look in her eye, just smiled.

A week later, when I saw that guy, it was difficult, but I know now that if I hadn't faced fears back at the lake, I never would have been able to face him with the full force of who I was that day. And more importantly, I now had the realization that it was never about a "him," it was always about a "me," learning to live my moments. Learning to unfreeze my stupid fears. Learning to listen to that little wise, crystal-clear voice when it whispers, "Go! Jump in that beautiful lake!" Learning the lesson to allow myself to open up and bloom *just because* and not get tied up in the whys and what ifs and buts and blah blah boring blahs.

I've met that wise little whisper many times since then. And it's never let me down. It appears out of nowhere, in the darkest of moments, ready to break me out of my own prison of fears and doubts. It never judges, only gently lights the way out of the maze. Maybe that's the same voice a flower hears just before it blooms. I'd like to think it is. That we are all gently cheered on by an inner knowing that is somehow unique to us, yet we, all manifestations of spirit, share.

Every day that we make a choice to be who we want to be and not let fear freeze us, is a day we get closer to God, the universe, all living creatures, and pretty importantly, our own selves. Over time, I have also learned that there is no wrong answer, or wrong path. If there's a lesson you need to learn, you can be sure the universe will continue putting forth the crossroads. And if you fail to heed the little voice of wisdom, no worries, always remember, "There's still time to change the road you're on."

Ilse Noir grew up in a small town in the American Southwest where there were "always more stars than people." She has since lived in Los Angeles and London, and now happily resides with her husband on a hill alongside a river in Europe.

Jumping into a natural body of mountain water lifts the spirit. It's like pressing a RESET button: you go in the water feeling one way, and exit renewed. Plan to press your own RESET this summer. Select a river or lake; mark the calendar; and make your plan. Come back later to write about your experience.

"Compassion practice is daring.
It involves learning to relax and allowing
ourselves to move gently toward what
scares us. The trick to doing this is to
stay with emotional distress without
tightening into aversion, to let fear soften
us, rather than harden into resistance."

~ Pema Chödrön

What I Never Expected

On a cool April day, a close friend fielded my questions about motherhood as her toddler leapt from stone to stone nearby. I gazed up at cottonwood trees, stroked my pregnant belly, and told her my plan.

"I'm going to strap my baby to my chest and hike into the woods right away," I announced, "Like hours after birth. I mean, women do it all over the world, right?"

"Yeah, but your vagina might hurt for a few weeks," she said.

Somehow, I hadn't ever considered that possibility. As a girl, I had hung upside down from tree branches and run faster than the boys. I grew into a woman of physical endurance — long bike races, long hikes, and long stretches of manual labor, building projects. After birth, my plan was simply to pull on my old jeans and get on with it. But my pregnancy had been rough. The nausea didn't go away after the first trimester. I became a pro at vomiting into a mason jar every day while driving to/from anywhere. It was, at times, demoralizing. I complained and yet told myself the intensity had prepared me for birth.

Labor, well, labor I would do a thousand times over. I touched into my wisest animal self — all breath and moan. No fear surfaced, even in pain, even when my home-water-birth turned into a van ride to the hospital as my midwife straddled me, held an oxygen mask to my face and requested that I don't push yet, even though the urge was strong. I ended up pushing for five hours until my umbilical-wrapped daughter came out. She wasn't the blue, breathless baby they expected. We were okay. I could have dropped to the floor and done 100 push-ups on the adrenaline of my empowerment. One nurse lifted her arms and said, "You were amazing! Look, I sweated through my scrubs. That was awesome."

Pregnancy may have knocked me over, but I had labored like Wonder Woman. If the upswing trajectory followed, postpartum would be manageable, maybe even a breeze.

Within a week, it was clear that the liquid coming out of me was no longer the standard lochia but urine. And not just when I sneezed. When I walked to the mailbox. When I squatted to pick up an errant sock. When I bounced to soothe my daughter to sleep. I was officially incontinent. I bought a Costco-size box of *Always* extra-long pads with wings and pasted one in my underwear at all times.

Maybe this problem would go away.

But it didn't.

I went hiking anyway.

I strapped my daughter to my chest and peed all over myself, through my pad, onto my shorts, onto the trail. My car seat smelled of urine, no matter how hard I scrubbed it. I learned to wear a skirt so other hikers wouldn't notice. When my new mama friends couldn't believe this was my new normal, I learned to make it normal.

"Oop, peed on myself again," I would laugh.

But the grief pressed against my face, my mouth, my neck. I refused to acknowledge it. I couldn't. I couldn't do that and everything else. There was so much everything else in new motherhood.

One afternoon, at a museum, my birth class friend had to carry both our children up the stairs because being pee-soaked in a museum isn't as acceptable as on the trail. I watched her strong arms and strong back and the sorrow of this comparison dug a groove through my heart. If I hadn't been in a public place, I would have collapsed. Would I never be able to carry my daughter up stairs? Where was I? Why couldn't I pull it together? Where was the woman who had labored without fear, almost without effort?

This went on for six months, for a year.

I saw some pelvic physical therapists. They looked at me with kind doe-eyes and gave me elaborated Kegel exercises. I did them solidly for a week. Maybe they were actually helping. At my cousin's wedding, I couldn't wait to dance. It had been so long. When I hit my first hip thrust/bounce, urine poured down my leg and almost onto the dance floor. I scuttled outside under the moon. There, alone, I could release my sobs. This was not what I had expected for our first evening out alone. Later that night, I begged my husband to suck the milk out of my breasts because they were so engorged without my daughter there to nurse them. So he did — in the dark of the parking lot with the car windows down, the smell of sagebrush on the night air. "It's sweet," he said, and we laughed, because the gap between laughing and crying was invisible. I woke desperate in the early morning. No breast pump. Hand expressing would not be fast enough. I grabbed my own large, painful breast and drank my own sweet milk. Urine or milk. Life is about fluids or being fluid, I think.

In the haze of sleep-deprivation, I couldn't manage a plan to do my pelvic floor exercises. All I could do was lie on the concrete floor and stare at the ceiling fan, the red latex PT strap unused. One morning, I woke unable to move. "Help," I gulped to my husband as he made his way out the door, "Help me." My battery had died and I couldn't lift my daughter. I watched her watch me with wide eyes. Panic washed over me in waves. A blood test revealed postpartum hypothyroidism on the edge of becoming an autoimmune condition. I morphed from someone who never took prescription medicine to someone who did. Healing this thyroid issue would also require, in part, more exercise, but every time I exercised, I peed. Sometimes I found myself in the woods throwing, no hurling, rocks at a tree. How had I gotten there? My rage scared me enough to request more blood tests. No serotonin problem, no postpartum depression, but my neurotransmitters were all off. Months later, adrenal fatigue became part of the picture. My doctor started an email to me with, "Dearest Molly, ..."

None of this was the worst thing possible.

None of this was a death sentence.

But I didn't believe it would ever change.

This was not the mother or woman I had ever wanted to be.

Every day I scanned my perimeter for someone to blame — my husband, my mother, my father, my friends, my dog, myself. My anger became volcanic. During the day, I sang, swam, laughed, loved, and smooched my daughter. When she fell asleep, I paced the kitchen and drove down dark roads at 1:00 a.m. fantasizing about walking into the woods and never returning. Was this what giving up looked like? But my daughter kept me accountable. I could never have left her. I made gratitude lists. There was so much to be grateful for. Hard as I tried, my gratitude practice fell flat.

Two years into this situation, something changed.

I don't know what clicked. I began to swim laps at our local hot springs. There I could exercise and pee and no one would know. At my doctor's suggestion, I stopped nursing and took progesterone and herbs. My daughter started to sleep through the night. As she potty-trained, I chanced it and stopped using pads every day. We could let go of diapers together. Summer came around again. Sun. Heat. Green. Maybe it helped that time had passed. I don't really know. I still wonder how nothing changed, but everything did. Maybe I decided to step back from the edge.

I decided.

I decided.

I decided.

For the first time in 35-years of living, I decided to be kind to myself. I started to talk to myself the way I talked to my daughter. "It's okay, I know it's hard, you can do it, do you need a hug, I see your radiance, I see you, I see you…"

When a body-worker recently told me that my pelvis was in shock and all tangled up, I didn't catastrophize with images of doom. I let her words pass out of me and replaced them with "my body is healing". I could cultivate this belief — despite the externals. Of course, this story is still alive. This, right now, is me finding my way. I still pee on myself, but mostly just before my period. I still take thyroid and adrenal medicine and may have to for who knows how long. But I'm off progesterone.

And now, I wouldn't want any part of my continuing journey to be different. It forced me to break up with my beloved anger. That, it turns out, was the only way to open the starting gates to heal. My righteous self used to quietly judge the hell out of people who make poor, life-altering decisions. Now I understand that we all walk an edge, whether we touch it or not. My pelvis is my new gal pal. We talk every day. I've gotten comfy with the mess of life. I've learned that grief can take time. The laboring woman in me has been laboring all along. She is the woman I was looking for. And this is the only way I could have found her.

Molly Caro May is a writer whose work explores body, place, and the foreign. She leads writing workshops across the country and her work has appeared in Orion Magazine, Salon, *and* Fourth Genre, *among others. Her memoir,* The Map of Enough: One Woman's Search For Place *(Counterpoint Press), was published in 2014. She lives with her husband and daughter in Bozeman, Montana where she is co-founder of the Thunderhead Writers' Collective. Her next book explores emotional inheritance through the matrilineal lineage.*

How do you tend to respond mentally or emotionally when your body becomes incapable, even if temporarily, of doing "the usual"? Think about an illness, injury, surgical procedure, or physical recuperation you've endured. What was the hardest part about that for you? Write a reassuring message to yourself, now that you have a little distance. Then, return to read this whenever you experience physical hardship again.

"You can't shake hands with a clenched fist."

~ Indira Gandhi

ANNE SINGER

Of Men, a Machine, and One Pretty Cool Moment

You live in a city like New York long enough and you learn to ignore things. The urban cacophony — sirens, horns, music, and that relentless commentary on you and the body you walk around in. You know, those verbal flares men send up that illuminate you in the crowd and alert everyone to the woman over here with the audacity to unbind her feet and venture out into the public spaces men think they own.

I have been asked by complete strangers, men passing on the street, *Why are you wearing that baggy jacket that covers you up? Where are you hurrying that's so important? Do you have a boyfriend?* At newsstands and markets, men behind the counter have seized my hand when counting back my change, locked eyes and smiled lasciviously while asking for my number. And I can't even count the number of times male passersby, store clerks, or strangers in restaurants have asked me why I won't smile for them. *Why are you so serious, baby? Smile!*

When I was living in New York, the most celebrated hecklers, the men most likely to remind you most loudly that it's their world and not yours, were construction workers. Maybe it was the mob-like nature of their commentary that made them notorious. Or maybe it was their primitive vocalizations of grunts and hollers and that piercing tongue trill. But when a crew of them set their sights on you and sent up their call, you began to feel like the sickly gazelle at the back of the herd who'd been spotted by the cheetah, so you put down your head and picked up your pace. At least, that's what I always did.

Until the day I didn't.

I was back in my Michigan hometown, a college town where intellect is prized, and gender bias, though endemic, is well controlled by healthy doses of liberalism. It's the kind of small city where a girl can almost grow up believing she is equal to men. I suppose there was a sense of safety for me, being back in such a tolerant little place after so many years in New York where gender, race, and wealth form a brittle template that seems to define just about every interaction.

It was a balmy July evening, and I was strolling downtown with my old best friend from high school. Dating back to the ninth grade, I had walked like this with Wendy through shopping malls and high school halls and along these same downtown streets. And although I can remember both the drama and the joy of being teenaged best friends, what I remember most vividly is the reflections of our two selves in every window glass we passed: Wendy, the tiny, adorable, and utterly feminine one with perfectly feathered hair; and me, the tallish, heavyish, lumbering one with her hair pulled back tight in a band or barrette. I saw myself as Big Bird. Wendy was the gorgeous guest host who makes Kermit swoon.

But now, in our 30s, that mirror image had changed, and I was learning to enjoy the way I looked in a pair of jeans. And, apparently, on that July evening, so did a crew of construction workers resurfacing a downtown parking lot.

As we passed their worksite, their call went up and the flares went off and sounds began to issue from the men as they turned away from their work and toward we two women in our summer sandals. But amidst the unintelligible chorus came a string of words in the form of a question: *You wanna' take a ride?* One of the men was pointing at one of the machines. It was massive, easily 10 feet off the ground, with a shiny hot steel cylinder nearly as high that slowly rolled across the sticky black asphalt in a fog of tarry steam. He asked again, *You wanna' take a ride?* and gestured at the seat high atop this mechanical monster.

And apparently, on that particular summer evening, I did want to take a ride.

I turned off the sidewalk and walked towards these hard-hatted men — to their utter delight, it seemed. They turned off their equipment, ceremoniously pulled back the sawhorse barricades, and cheered me on as I entered their hot working world. When I stepped onto the plywood planks that crossed the lot, I looked back and saw Wendy standing there, hands clasped tight, just below her slack-jawed smile.

I don't remember how I actually mounted the rolling machine, but somehow I found myself sitting up high, next to its driver as it rumbled and jolted and began to move. We took a few runs across the lot, back and forth in the kind of pattern you see combines travel at harvest time.

I have to tell you, it was exhilarating! The sheer scale and power of the machine beneath me gave me a glimpse into what makes men and boys stop and marvel at the cranes and bulldozers at construction sites. I also have to tell you, it was a little bit scary, so I remained firmly seated rather than stand up, as a different woman might have done, and wave my arms in some gesture of liberated abandon.

As I've shared this story with friends, however, I've come to think that a different woman might not have accepted this invitation in the first place — let alone spread her arms like Kate Winslet in "Titanic." And this surprises me.

What surprises me is that I, of all people, the one with the baggy jacket and the Big Bird stride would seize this moment and turn a sexual taunt into a moment of, I guess, joy. And surely, that man in the caution-yellow vest didn't really want me to ride his roller, did he?

Back in my New York days, I was once walking along with a girlfriend, beautiful Lydia. An older, disheveled man passing by muttered that she should stop and give him some time. So, she stopped. And then she turned around and yelled, *You want me stop, old man? You want to drop your pants so I can give you a blow job right here on the sidewalk? Is that what you want? Well, c'mon then!* The man just kept walking.

Men don't really mean it when they ask you to stop, to give them a smile or a phone number or take a ride on their heavy machinery. When men make these requests, they are really just singling us out, seeking to intimidate, flagging women as trespassers in the public spaces they dominate.

But it's also true that we don't always have to let them. The older I get, the more I realize this is true. And the more I wish for all women to know confidence, to experience safety, and to seize a little more joy.

After living most of her adult life in New York and Washington, DC, Anne Singer now lives in rural Virginia, where she writes about policy from her home office with pink walls.

A prompt from Anne: Think about the number of times we walk away from a situation wishing we'd said something clever . . . write about one of those situations, and imagine three things you might have said.

"A bird doesn't sing because it has an answer,
it sings because it has a song."

~ Joan Walsh Anglund

KRISTIN MCCLOY

A Novel Idea

If anybody asks, as everybody does, I am a writer. I've dabbled with plays, poetry, published a couple of stories, written some reviews, edited other people's work, and taught; but mostly, I'm a novelist, and very lucky that when my first one was finished, I was in the right place at the right time (young/NYC/late '80s, with a runaway manuscript that had five sex scenes, not a single one gratuitous).

Velocity made me a ridiculous amount of money while my second novel had already been bought as an *idea*. Because of this, I fell, and for too long remained under the illusion that writing would always sustain me.

HA!

My third novel, *Hollywood Savage*, published by an imprint of Simon & Schuster called Atria Books was given zero publicity. They rushed it out without even the author photo I had provided, or any blurbs from other authors. Perhaps they decided I would make a better tax deduction, but it was very hard to watch something I'd spent several years on come and go without a trace.

I am now working on my fourth novel, advance-free and editor-less.

All of the above is the preamble to the how and why I became an animal caretaker.

Primarily, it is something I do to generate some cash flow, if not much, but it *is* all cash, and boy does it flow. In and right back out again — as it should! That's why it's called currency.

I've been stupid rich, and I've been astonishingly poor, and I've discovered that I'm not materialistic, and I don't need more money than it takes for me to live on — which I've learned to do with not much, unless you don't count on tremendous generosity from your friends — and I do. Oh boy, do I!

In fact, part of that help began when a woman I met at my first reading for Litquake, and who became the most constant member of my fiction workshop, asked if I would consider staying in their back storage unit/living studio to take care of their menagerie (one dog and three cats, plus the house and garden), so that she and her husband could take a three-month fellowship he'd landed in Marseilles, France.

The storage unit is filled mostly with books, has a wonderfully high bed, high ceilings, great insulation and a skylight, while the garden is lush and wild, with plum and apple and peach trees, along with a lot of fennel which attracts Monarch and Swallowtail butterflies. I couldn't say yes fast enough, especially when I saw that my own kitty, Zelly, a serious hunter, could leap out the window and into the mysterious natural world whenever she wanted, and then back in again — I felt like I'd won the lottery.

After they returned and graciously allowed me to stay on, I looked for more animal caretaking jobs and slowly began acquiring clients, two of whom book me at the beginning of every year, and who've kept me afloat when other jobs occasionally dried up.

While the work is not exactly high-pay, I love it — not least because it comes so easily to me, as I've loved animals with a freakish intensity ever since I was a little girl, as I think most children do (just look at picture books!) Innocence has such a soft spot for other innocence, and children are particularly vulnerable, as are nearly all the animals in our world.

I'm good at what I do because I have never not fallen in love with other people's animals. It's fun getting to know each little sentient being for its own distinct personality, with as many quirks and differing habits as any person I know. The exception is that, given enough time and attention, all of these little guys will start to shower me with affection in their own way — whether it's wanting to be in (literal) touch at all times, or deciding they need to sleep on my chest at 3:00 a.m. Some of them follow me from room to room, others are more, Can you open the effing door already?

Like Jules Feiffer's cartoon women, I dance to the ever-present grace in every single cat, their ability to drape themselves anywhere (and then sleep!) to twist themselves while free-falling in space so as to land on their flexible feet, then simply walk away unscathed (and, more importantly to them, I believe, unembarrassed!)

I dance to the way they pretend you don't matter, but manage to keep you in their sight-lines at all times, regardless of how well they hide themselves (it's called 'cat space' and if that cat does not want to be found, well then: good luck!)

When I'm writing I often ask my small charges to help me channel the genie, and so often they will curl up around me (on the arm of a couch, on the floor at my feet, nearby on a windowsill) and fall into the trance-like sleep I so envy, creating an atmosphere of deep serenity into which my mind can drop.

The only thing I dislike about animal care is that I have to leave Zelly at home by herself, where she basically just waits for me. She's an Abyssinian, a breed known for their wild beauty as well as their unusual loyalty. They bond with a single being and you, lucky lucky you, become their world.

I got Zelly after the cat I had adopted from a neighbor who was never home — a regal creature I named Napoleon — was hit by some asshole driving very fast down a single-block street. Napoleon tried to come home and made it only halfway across the street. I bent over him and howled. The grief was so intense I knew the only thing that would help would be adopting another cat, because believe me, there is no shortage of beings who need out of a cage and into your heart.

Zelly was curious, insanely playful, and if you threw something for her, she would snatch it out of thin air and bring it back. Not like a dog, panting and leaving it at your feet, but much more casually, jumping on the bed and carelessly dropping it near your hand. Her cool was stunning, and very funny. But when she needed affection, she let me know. She would get up on my chest and knead me, then curl up next to me and sling one paw over my collarbone. I often fell asleep holding that paw.

Somewhere along the line, I had the realization that my cat was essentially living for me. Attending to her own cat business (oh where to take those seventeen naps?), but also waiting for me to come home, wanting attention, wanting to play, and later, if I'm very lucky, jumping in bed when I wake up panicked by everything at 5:00 a.m. to meow in my face then curl up in the space between arm and heart to purr us both back to sleep.

Understanding that this breathing, living, loving, very chatty being was and is singularly devoted to me struck me with a sudden force. The extent of that devotion left me breathless, and from then on, I knew: she wasn't my cat, I was her girl.

I think most people take their animals' utter devotion for granted, and I want to shake them and ask, Don't you understand what an honor that is?

So here's the thing: while I identify myself as a writer, a label that goes a lot deeper than words (no pun etc.), who's to say what's the more important work? Writing books that one hopes will outlast one's own lifetime, and might perhaps achieve what Jean Cocteau always claimed was the main reason for writing — to "utterly overwhelm a single soul"? Or is it the care and love that flows between myself and the animals I've been entrusted with, including my own?

I met a dog named Dirk when I was an undergraduate at Duke. Dirk was easily the smartest animal I've ever met (she should have been, considering how many classes she attended with me alone!) She was one of my roommates during her owner's last semester at the university, and when I asked for custody, her human sneered and said, You don't even know where you're going to live next year!

Well, that was true. But apparently, Dirk did. Because one day, when I wasn't even home, my sister, with whom I shared an off-campus house along with a litany of others, heard a wild scratching on the screen door, opened it, and in out of the rain came Dirk. She jumped on the couch, stretched out, and fell asleep. She remembered my promise, and she obviously had my number. For the rest of the time I was there, Dirk lived with me.

When, we had to part, I entrusted her with my soul. She was the fiercest guard I could think of, and when I die, I pray she will be the first creature I see. And when I look around, I hope that I see every other animal I ever loved, freed, helped, took care of, or mourned for — including every animal sacrifice, any animal hurt, wounded, or poached — every animal in the whole wide world.

Because that is my idea of Heaven.

This essay is a shout out to the gorgeous variety of creatures who have their own deep intelligence, and everything to teach us about being at ease in your own skin, trusting your instincts, and loving without limit.

*Kristin McCloy is a thrice-published author (*Velocity, Some Girls, *and* Hollywood Savage)*, working on her fourth, and living in Oakland with the cat who owns her, Zelly, and the family who took them in.*

Think about the pets and animals you've known. How have they helped provide a beneficial perspective on how to live your own life?

"The trouble with the rat race is that even if you win, you're still a rat."

~ Lily Tomlin

KAREN WOLF-SCHNEIDER

Go With the Flow

My life's headlines might read like a *National Enquirer* front page: "KILLER BEES ATTACK SAILORS IN VENEZUELAN JUNGLE" or "HURRICANE FLOYD SWAMPS COUPLE IN NEW JERSEY MARSHES" or "SOUTH PACIFIC STORM TESTS SAILOR'S SKILLS." These splashy headlines describe events through which I've tested my abilities to be fabulously daring while sailing around the world in a 38-foot sailboat. Sure, I've experienced fearful events and lonely hours when I've had to find the inner strength to pull through, but the key to these adventures was a willingness to change, to leave my safe and comfortable lifestyle, and to dare to do something completely different. All because of a butterfly.

This story starts in 1993 when I was a 34-year-old divorcee, homeowner, and landscape architect, contentedly living and working in northern California. I lived alone in a home that I loved and with a job that gave me creative independence. I had a good circle of friends and felt content with my life. I was quick to say "yes," however, when my folks invited me to join them for a week of timeshare vacation on the island of St. Maarten, an alluring destination in the eastern Caribbean. I looked forward to white, sandy beaches and time with my parents, whom I had seldom seen since their move down south.

The week after that, I would go on a solo dive adventure in the crystal blue waters of the Virgin Islands, for which the Caribbean is famous.

The timeshare was a dream hotel with lovely, breezy rooms and a large balcony overlooking the beach of Great Bay. The curving crescent of sand was backed by a multitude of sailboats anchored in the turquoise water. Daily activities were all organized by a woman named Helen, who was about my age and who quickly became a friend. One night after a catamaran "sunset cruise," she and I went to the marina for dinner and drinks. After dinner, a rocking dance beat drew our attention to the dockside bar, which was crowded with a motley assortment of boaters and water-oriented locals.

We sat at the bar, joining in the revelry of the funky band whose music had everyone in the mood to party. When it came time for an audience-participation number, folks were hooting and hollering, knocking their beer mugs on the table in beat to the rhythm whenever their group was called out: "all the women clap your hands," "all you fellows stomp your feet," "everybody with orange hair swing to the beat." Or, something like that. (I would have tried to remember the song, had I known that it was bound to change the course of my life.)

The distinguished-looking fellow to my left kept knocking his glass on the table, no matter which group was being singled-out. Jovially, I turned to him and asked if perhaps I should tell him when to knock.

"*Schuldigung*," he said to me. (Obviously, this guy was not fluent in English.)

"Oh, sorry," I said. "Thought you might need some help interpreting. My name is Karen. Where are you from?"

"My name is Horst," he replied. "I am from Austria, and I am here on my boat, waiting for the right weather to cross the Atlantic and return to my home sea, the Mediterranean."

Our chance encounter that night led to an invitation to sail on his boat *Flow*. Of course, since this was a family vacation, my parents had to be included. And so, we sailed. We then proceeded to have dinner at the timeshare, lunch at a little Chinese Restaurant, and a drive around the island in our rental car. It was almost as if Horst was already a member of the family. Sadly, our week together was coming to an end and I was flying on to the British Virgin Islands (BVI) for my dive.

"Don't fly," said Horst. "Let's sail there together."

How could I pass up an opportunity like that? We said goodbye to my folks and set sail into the sunset for a nighttime passage to Tortola, BVI. I had sailed the San Francisco Bay a few times with friends, and had done some small-boat sailing on lakes as a kid, but I had never been out at night, out of sight of land, or with anyone who used English as a second language to command our navigation. Some things got lost in translation, but I did learn that "fock" is a German name for sail, and a "sheet" is the rope you use to tighten the fock. Horst and I laughed a lot about the misunderstandings that inevitably occurred in our mixed German-English-Spanish vocabulary, and we spent a delightful week exploring the coastline and diving the rocks and wrecks of the beautiful island waters.

When I awoke in my parents' house the first night after returning to the U.S., the billowing curtains had become sails, and the soft spring breeze, a Caribbean caress. But I was back in the States and it was time for me to fly home and my old workaday reality.

Horst and I continued our romance by fax, which helped us rediscover the art of letter writing. It's interesting what we reveal in the written word. Horst was lonely single-handing his sailboat, but decided he wasn't ready to return to Europe. Instead, he would spend another year as a charter skipper, sailing with guests from Europe aboard his sailboat, teaching astral navigation and sailing technique. I was alone in a big house, working hard to maintain a life in the big city, and wondering what I was doing, getting involved with an older man from a different culture who was living the life of a gypsy in the eastern Caribbean. Our letters to each other described such different worlds. Nevertheless, we found ourselves growing closer and more comfortable with each other as we shared funny anecdotes about the events in our lives.

Several months passed and the stack of letters grew taller. I was turning 35, an age at which I had always envisioned myself as being settled, at least married, maybe with a child or two. Instead, I was single with a mortgage and a car that had another year's worth of payments before it was truly mine. When Horst invited me to spend my birthday sailing the outer islands of Venezuela, I really did have to think twice. It's not easy acting irresponsibly when you're almost middle-aged.

I flew into Caracas. Settled high on a plateau where the Andes plunge down to the Caribbean Sea, the city was a striking contrast to the remote, sandy islets of Los Aves, a coral-encrusted natural reserve 80 miles across the sea, which was to be our sailing destination.

We shopped for a few provisions at the local *tienda* (shop): papaya, mango, potatoes, cabbage, onions, garlic, and beer. The fish we would catch ourselves. The limited refrigeration meant that anything else would come from a can. We took a long shower at the marina before casting off, because the limited water supply meant that fresh-water showers would be mostly in the rain.

We were heading for virtually uninhabited, barely charted, little specks of land across a deep sea probably infested with pirates, and we were armed with nothing more than a bottle opener and a fishing spear. The weather report mentioned a tropical disturbance east of the area, but that kind of thing is barely noted in Venezuela where hurricanes are only a little more frequent than snow in the Amazon.

Horst and I spent the days and nights in an intimacy that is rarely found elsewhere, two people alone together on a small, floating platform, surrounded by nothing but water, coral reefs, and an occasional sandy hill. We swam, fished, cooked, and talked, made love, and talked some more. Days went by with no human contact, only the radio voices that talked about the heavy, windless weather that becalmed us halfway back to the mainland.

When Horst asked if I would like to live with him on the boat, I was both intrigued and uncertain. Traveling by boat could be a great way to explore the world, but would I have much opportunity if I were "crew" on a charter boat? Someone has to do all the cleaning, shopping, and cooking. Charter guests are probably interesting to meet, but do I really want to live with strangers for two weeks at a time on a sailboat? And what about when there are no guests? Can I live with another person in a place where taking a walk to "cool off" means jumping into the ocean? Plus, what about my house, my car, my job?

I settled on the foredeck of *Flow* in the shade of the sails which were beginning to fill with a freshening breeze, my thoughts filled with contemplation of the future. What should I do? How could I set aside all that I had worked so hard to achieve for an uncertain adventure? Could I change my lifestyle and my attitudes to endure moderate deprivation? Our relationship was good now, but what might happen when we really got to know each other? As I looked broodingly across my toes at the darkening horizon, a tiny yellow butterfly landed gently on my foot. It shook its wings, silently danced across my toes, and settled down as if for a conversation. I smiled and listened.

Suddenly, Horst came forward from the cockpit. The voices on the radio now sounded an alarm: perhaps that far-off tropical depression is deepening into a tropical storm. It looks like it is going to hit Caracas. Perhaps it's headed our way. Perhaps we'd better hurry-up and find a safe place.

We started the engine and plotted a course to the nearest port where I could eventually catch a bus back to Caracas and my flight home. Horst would then hurry to the deepest lagoon to secure himself and the boat against the incoming storm.

Six months later, I moved aboard. How long would it last? Six days, six weeks, six years? In the past twelve years, we have sailed from Venezuela to Boston, Florida to Panama, San Diego to Tahiti. We've lived for periods of time in Austria, Maryland, and California, and I've been blessed to see the world at a truly leisurely pace. We've also faced many storms together, both physical and personal; this sailing life isn't always easy, and it's not for everyone. But I am happy I took a chance to change my life.

I'll never forget that yellow butterfly. It said, "If butterflies are free, you can be too. Go with the *Flow*!"

The sailing life has taken Karen halfway around the world and back again. She spent a decade in the "Middle Earth," where she found a community of friends and family in New Zealand who would have remained strangers had she not decided to "go with the Flow." She and Horst are now back in California exploring the States in a land yacht.

A prompt from Karen: "Do you believe there are signs from the universe that can help direct your destiny? I do!!" Write about those signs, and how they've steered you.

"Act boldly and unseen forces
will come to your aid."

~ Dorothea Brande

DORIS "GRANNY D" HADDOCK

Walking Across America in My 90th Year

Jim and I, at long last, got in the vehicle and drove home to Dublin, New Hampshire. My, it was delicious to see the miles fly by and not have to even think about walking them! And then my town ahead, and there it is! And the old house! My old chair! Bathtub! Books! Ahh, my tired bones!

On Tuesday morning I made my way back to my old friends — our Tuesday Morning Academy. They were happy to see me, but it was rather as if I had been ill for a time or off on a cruise. Within a few minutes, I was one of the girls again — except for one difference. One of my friends, after a few minutes of conversation about my walk, said she didn't see what was so important about campaign finance reform.

It is reported that I took her rather sharply to task with a presentation of memorable ferocity. Well, was that me? Old Doris? It was not the Doris who had sat meekly among them a year and a quarter earlier. Even at my age, I had changed quite a bit.

For the first time in my long life, I was clearly not afraid of what someone might think of me — I cared more about the issue than my vain self. That transition was worth the walk, though I must keep working on it.

Several weeks later I received a call. A group of campaign finance reformers from the Alliance for Democracy were going into the Capitol Rotunda to petition for the redress of our grievance against campaign corruption. Yes, I said — I would go with them this time. I could care less anymore if people thought I was crazy. This was a way to push the issue forward — to demonstrate the depth of our concern and to take the pain of social change upon ourselves.

So I returned to Washington. On the evening of April 20, 2000, I walked from a train at Union Station to a church building near the Supreme Court. There I was to meet thirty-one others who would risk arrest. I was a bit late, as the streets of Washington can be confusing. I entered a room where the thirty-one were seated in chairs gathered in a great circle, and my perilous seat waited empty for me.

In the few steps across the room, I reminded myself that my whole life had been spent worrying too much about what others thought about me. Go ahead, old girl, have a seat.

It was a comfortably well-worn chair, and I looked around with wonder at the smiling people around me, bathed as they were in the golden light of the old room. Many had lost themselves to their causes many years ago. Some, like me, were young beginners.

I was arrested the next morning for reading the Declaration of Independence in a calm voice in the Rotunda. I did so to make the point that we must declare our independence from campaign corruption. My wrists were pulled behind me and cuffed. I was taken away to jail along with the others. When you jump fully into the river of your values, every moment glows with a blissful joy, even when your arms hurt behind you.

But, oh, dear husband, Jim! Are you up there looking down, laughing at me in the pokey? Get used to it, dear.

The fear of not being liked — of not belonging — has been central in my life. "She's not like the others. She's different. Sometimes I wonder if she's mine at all, like I found her in a basket on my front doorstep," I overheard my mother say when I was seven.

Not knowing how else to proceed, I embraced the idea that I was different. I was a princess in disguise. The pink granite Laconia

Public Library, complete with turret, became my castle, and I read every adventure book in it. At home, my nose was always in a book until Mama scolded me to do my chores.

That overheard conversation, and that uncertainty helped me to become well-read and adventurous, which has made me a connoisseur of life and of people. It has sent me on a lifetime of adventures — I can't imagine how boring I might have otherwise become to others and to myself.

It does help to know that I was, in fact, loved. At Sybil's wake, when a priest asked Mama who would be taking care of her now that Sybil was gone, Mama's eyes brightened with joy when I said, "Why, she will be coming to live with me, won't you, Mama?" It may have been only the sparkle of an extinguished worry, but I have clung to it.

Do we see who we are, finally? Do we see, behind the curtain, the scars and the insecurities that have controlled us? And when we see them and look them squarely in the eye, do they lose their power over us, backing down from their bullying bluster? Indeed they do. We become free to take our lie in whatever shape it has become, and find a good and enjoyable use for it, serving others and ourselves.

Interesting! After all this chattering, I have not told you five minute's worth about my long career in the shoe industry. For so many years, that was all I could think about, and now it hardly seems worth bringing up. I think the lesson there is that a career, in the end, is a much smaller part of our lives than we can possibly imagine at the time. Our career distracts us from our real work, so we must learn to see past the limits of that blinkered world. All those years condense now in my mind to a chuckle.

The aftermath of my arrest was that I was later brought before the judge in Washington for my crime of being a troublesome person. While I hoped he would not put an old woman in jail for six months for reading the Declaration of Independence in the Capitol, as well he could, I yet worried that perhaps all of this, all of me, had been silly and he would now send me away to contemplate my silliness for a few months. As he sat expressionless in his great robe, I wondered what this wise-looking old man thought.

Judge Hamilton finally spoke, and most mercifully. He sentenced me, and the others, to the time we had already served, and he added these words of heavenly grace:

"As you know, the strength of our great country lies in its Constitution and her laws and in her courts. But more fundamentally, the strength of our great country lies in the resolve of her citizens to stand up for what is right when the masses are silent. And, unfortunately, sometimes it becomes the lot of the few, sometimes like yourselves, to stand up for what's right when the masses are silent."

His honor gave me a fine hug in his chambers afterward. His staff members were tearful and I was tearful, and America felt like my own country again.

So I am happy for how my walk has turned out, and for how my life has turned out. I am thankful for the troubles that have shaped me. If you and I were having a cup of tea and you were telling me your stories, as I have told you mine, I would see that it was your hard times that made you so interesting, so wise and able to laugh at life. Aren't we lucky, friend, to be the creatures of such a genius Creator that even our darkest troubles graciously serve to deepen and wide our hearts? And all our memories, like days cast in amber, glow more beautifully through the years as the happy endings finally reveal themselves and flow slowly into the bright and mysterious river of the Divine.

Well, I am not finished . . . with my life or with my passion for campaign finance reform. There is almost always time to find another victory, another happy ending. I hope that is your feeling about life, too.

Doris "Granny D" Haddock received a lot of attention when she walked across the country, campaigning to raise awareness for campaign finance reform. She likely received more attention for being an 89-year-old grandmother attempting this feat, and she knew this. She continued to speak publicly and travel the country for campaign finance reform until she passed away in 2010, six weeks after her 100th birthday.

Is there a cause you'd be willing to get arrested for? If you *have* been arrested while being active for a cause, what happened?

"Much love to everyone who is busy being a blessing."

~ Germany Kent

Acknowledgements

I am so very grateful for the support and encouragement I received while editing and publishing this book. Your enthusiasm, one and all, made a huge difference.

First and foremost, to ALL YOU WONDERFUL STORY CONTRIBUTORS: living with the pages of your personal stories was a constant uplift; a beautiful reminder of what it means to dare to be fabulous in all aspects of life. Communicating with each and every one of you through the editing process and beyond has been affirming and rewarding. Thanks for being you, for sharing your stories, and for making this book possible.

Patti Howard: the word "fabulous" didn't become a part of my vernacular until we met. You brought it. The spunk. The spirit. The verve. Our shared adventure ignited the spark of "DTBF!" and the original website. And now, years later, here I am with a book.

John McCloy: You rock; not just musically, but also artistically. Thank you for your generous assistance through the years, designing everything from logos and bookmarks to DVD covers (remember those?) and T-shirts.

Ellen Fagan, Donna Henderson-King, and Kristin McCloy: thank you for reading all previous stories on the website and providing sought-after feedback. Your notes and responses proved immensely helpful in selecting the stories for this book, and in considering some of the prompts.

Teddi Black: people most definitely judge a book by its cover. Thank you for manifesting my vision with the radiant cover of this book and the Journal Notebook. I love them.

Megan McCullough: You're simply wonderful. Thank you for taking my drafts and ideas and notes and turning them into beautiful book files.

John McKetta: the Universe conspired to connect me with the perfect proofreader. Your enthusiastic response to this book was truly reinforcing, and your notes and suggestions were everything I was hoping for, and then some.

Marko Vide: what can I say? You've been with DTBF from day one when you literally brought the website to life! I lucked out working with you. You are insightful, responsive, dependable, clear, and fun to work with. And you know how much I enjoy our philosophical exchanges. I value you as both a colleague and a friend.

Chris Ardito: *mi socia*! Your fresh perspective, professional eye for good design, and always-helpful suggestions truly kept me going with this project. Thanks for joining me on this journey and making the ride all the more enjoyable.

And finally, thank you, Henri Laborde, My Love: talk about supporting me from the very beginning! You helped me get out of my own way, while also providing an example of staying committed to good work. I will always be in awe of your keen eye for beautiful design. Thank you for everything. You are my rock, MSL. I love you.

Permissions & Citations

Stories

Alcoholic Anonymous. "The Fabulosity of Simplicity." Copyright ©2022 by the author. Published with permission from the author.

Burk, Penny Ross. "Fear City." Copyright ©2022 by Penny Ross Burk. Published with permission from the author.

Carrington, Terri Lyne. "Full Circle and Living an Authentic Life." Copyright ©2022 by Terri Lyne Carrington. Published with permission from the author.

Chaitowitz, Simon. "Playing the Cancer Card." Copyright ©2022 by Simon Chaitowitz and John Thomas. Published with permission from the author.

Chamaa, Rebecca. "Revealing My Secret: I Have Paranoid Schizophrenia." Copyright ©2022 by Rebecca Chamaa. Published with permission from the author.

Elkins, Anna. "'We Can Read!'" Copyright ©2022 by Anna Elkins. Published with permission from the author.

Haddock, Doris. "Walking Across America in My 90th Year." Excerpt from *Walking Across America in My Ninetieth Year* by Doris Haddock and Dennis Burke, Copyright ©2001 by Doris Haddock and Dennis Burke. Used by permission of Villard Books, an imprint of Random House, a division of Penguin Random House LLC. All rights reserved. Published with permission from the authors. Any third party use of this material, outside of this publication, is prohibited. Interested parties must apply directly to Penguin Random House LLC for permission.

Haynes, Melissa. "A Life-Long Dream Realized." Copyright ©2022 by Melissa Haynes. Published with permission from the author.

Helliwell, Carter. "Sola Pedaling." Copyright ©2022 by Carter Helliwell. Published with permission from the author.

Jolovitz, Jenna. "How I Found My Fabulous." Copyright ©2022 by Jenna Jolovitz. Published with permission from the author.

Levine, Alison. "On the Edge." Copyright ©2022 by Alison Levine. Published with permission from the author.

Longstalker, Pippy. "Roller Derby: The New Self-Help Sport." Copyright ©2022 by Laura Madson. Published with permission from the author.

Maggiora, Michele. "Ode to Gray." Copyright ©2022 by Michele Maggiora. Published with permission from the author.

May, Molly Caro. "What I Never Expected." Copyright ©2022 by Molly Caro May. Published with permission from the author.

McArthur, Jo-Anne. "Love Made Visible." Copyright ©2022 by Jo-Anne McArthur. Published with permission from the author.

McCloy, Johanna. "I Canceled My Wedding." Copyright ©2022 by Johanna McCloy. Published with permission from the author.

McCloy, Kristin. "A Novel Idea." Copyright ©2022 by Kristin McCloy. Published with permission from the author.

McCloy, Lillian. "Mrs. Spook." Excerpt from *Six Car Lengths Behind an Elephant: Undercover & Overwhelmed as a CIA Wife and Mother* by Lillian McCloy. Copyright ©2016 by Johanna McCloy. Reprinted with permission of Bordertown Publishing. All rights reserved. Published with permission from the author.

McKetta, Elisabeth Sharp. "Moist: A Journey Out of Chapstick Addiction." Copyright ©2022 by Elisabeth Sharp McKetta. Published with permission from the author.

Noir, Ilse. "How Does a Flower Dare to Bloom?" Copyright ©2022 by Ilse Noir. Published with permission from the author.

Robinson, Jill. "Her Name was Hong." Copyright ©2022 by Jill Robinson. Published with permission from the author.

Rushfield, Alexandra. "A Comedy Writer's Story." Copyright ©2022 by Alexandra Rushfield. Published with permission from the author.

Shaiq, Moina. "Meet a Muslim." Copyright ©2022 by Moina Shaiq. Published with permission from the author.

Singer, Anne. "Of Men and a Machine." Copyright ©2022 by Anne Singer. Published with permission from the author.

Steinem, Gloria. "On Self-Esteem." Published with permission from the author. Excerpt from *Revolution from Within: A Book of Self-Esteem* by Gloria Steinem. Copyright ©1992, 1993 by Gloria Steinem. Reprinted by permission of Little Brown and Company. All rights reserved.

Tokuda, Wendy. "A Shy TV Anchor." Copyright ©2022 by Wendy Tokuda. Published with permission from the author.

Wolf-Schneider, Karen. "Go with the Flow." Copyright ©2022 by Karen Wolf-Schneider. Published with permission from the author.

Quotations

Angelou, Maya. *Facebook.* 17 Feb. 2017. www.facebook.com/MayaAngelou/photos/a.485196574795.264196.33512954795/10155459929079796/?type=3.

Anglund, Joan Walsh. *A Cup of Sun: A Book of Poems.* Harcourt, Brace & World, 1967. *(Often attributed to Maya Angelou).*

Ball, Lucille. "Lucille Ball Biography." Biography.com Editors, *Biography.com,* A&E Television Networks, 24 Nov. 2011. www.biography.com/actor/lucille-ball.

Biles, Simone. *Twitter.* 10 May 2016, 9:37 p.m. www.twitter.com/simone_biles/status/730255395554365441?lang=en.

Brande, Dorothea. *Wake Up and Live!* Simon & Schuster, 1 Jan. 1980.

Brown, Brené. *Daring Greatly: How the Courage to Be Vulnerable Transforms the Way We Live, Love, Parent, and Lead.* Avery; Reprint edition, 7 Apr. 2015.

Chanel, Coco. *Believing in Ourselves.* Edited by Armand Eisen, Andrews McMeel Publishing; Miniature Book edition, 1 Jan. 1992.

Child, Lydia Maria. *Letters from New York: 1st and 2d Series.* London, F. Pitman., 1879, p. 232.

Chödrön, Pema. *Comfortable with Uncertainty: 108 Teachings on Cultivating Fearlessness and Compassion.* Shambhala Publications, 2008.

DeGeneres, Ellen. Tulane University Commencement Speech, 2009.

Gandhi, Indira. Press conference, New Delhi. 19 Oct. 1971. As cited in "Indian and Pakistani Armies Confront Each Other Along Borders" by Sydney H. Schanberg, *The New York Times,* 20 Oct. 1971, p. 6C. www.barrypopik.com/index.php/new_york_city/entry/you_cannot_shake_hands_with_a_clenched_fist.

Gibson, Althea. *I Always Wanted to Be Somebody*. HarperCollins, 1958.

Goodall, Jane. *My Life with the Chimpanzees*. Aladdin; Revised edition, 1 Apr. 1996.

Jackson, Glenda. *Popcorn in Paradise*. Edited by John Robert Colombo, Holt, Rinehart and Winston, 1 Jan. 1979.

Kaling, Mindy. *Twitter*. 8 June 2014. www.twitter.com/mindykaling/status/475515607698243584.

Kent, Germany. "Email Interview." Citation and permission provided by Germany Kent via email on 13 Apr. 2022.

Lichtenstein, Grace. "Competition in Women's Athletics." *Competition: A Feminist Taboo?* Edited by Valerie Miner and Helen E. Longino, The Feminist Press at the City University of New York, 1987.

Mayer, Katrina. *Instagram*. 6 Dec. 2013. www.instagram.com/p/hmLUcNOXQ7/?hl=en.

Morrison, Toni. *Song of Solomon*. Knopf Doubleday Publishing Group; Reprint edition, 8 June 2004.

Nin, Anais. *The Diary of Anais Nin, Vol. 3, 1939-1944*. Edited by Gunther Stuhlmann, Houghton Mifflin, 2009.

Onassis, Jacqueline Kennedy. *The Kennedys: An American Drama* by Peter Collier and David Horowitz, Encounter Books; 2nd edition, 1 Jan. 2002.

Ono, Yoko. "Yoko Ono Quotes." *IMDB.com*. Accessed 30 Apr. 2022. www.imdb.com/name/nm0648780/quotes.

Radner, Gilda. *It's Always Something*. HarperCollins, 1 Jan. 1990.

Reeves, Dianne. "Endangered Species." *Art & Survival*. EMI Records, 1993.

Roosevelt, Eleanor. *TheQuoteInvestigator.com*. As researched by Garson O'Toole, 30 Apr. 2012. www.quoteinvestigator.com/2012/04/30/no-one-inferior/.

Smith, Patti. *Early Work, 1970-1979*. W. W. Norton & Company; 2nd edition, 17 June 1995.

Stern, Jessica. *Denial: A Memoir of Terror*. Ecco Press, 2010, p. 137.

Tomlin, Lily. "Is This the Country to Whom I'm Speaking?" *People*, Volume 8, Number 26, Time Inc., 26 Dec. 1977.

Ulrich, Laurel Thatcher. "Vertuous Women Found: New England Ministerial Literature, 1668-1735". *American Quarterly*, 1976.

Welty, Eudora. *One Writer's Beginnings*. Harvard University Press, 1984, ch. 3.

Wilder, Laura Ingalls. *Little House in the Ozarks*. Bbs Pub Corp; 1st Galahad Books Ed edition, 1 Sep. 1996.

Winters, Shelley. *Wild Words from Wild Women*. Edited by Autumn Stevens, Conari Press; Revised edition, 1 Sep. 2014.

About the Editor

Johanna McCloy grew up internationally, living in Spain, India, Japan, and Venezuela before getting her B.A. in International Comparative Studies and Anthropology from Duke University. She is a published writer and editor, as well as an actor with starring and guest starring roles in theatre, television, and film. In addition to *Dare to be Fabulous*, Johanna edited her mother's highly-rated CIA memoir, *Six Car Lengths Behind an Elephant* by Lillian McCloy.

Johanna currently resides in the San Francisco Bay Area with her husband, Henri Laborde, a residential architect, and spends as much time as possible hiking in the Sierra, following the trails to her own true north.

"DTBF!"

Did you enjoy this book?

Reader ratings make a big difference to a small publisher and help other readers discover the book.

Please take a few minutes to rate this book on your book retailer or library website.

Thank you!

Would you like to receive occasional book-related updates from Bordertown Publishing?
Join our mailing list! https://eepurl.com/dAnbIL

For more information about Bordertown Publishing, please visit www.bordertownpublishing.com

Also from Bordertown Publishing

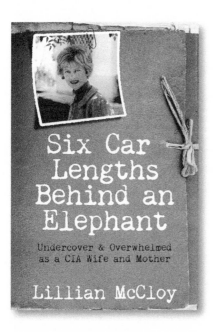

Six Car Lengths Behind
an Elephant: Undercover
& Overwhelmed as a CIA
Wife and Mother

By Lillian McCloy

*"A charming and unusual portrait
of the secret life." —John le Carré*

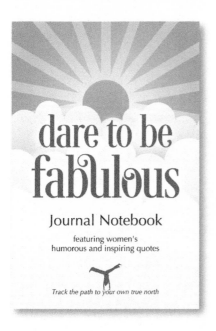

Dare to be Fabulous
Journal Notebook

Track the path to your own
true north.

*Glossy hardcover. 120 pages.
50+ quotes.*

Made in United States
North Haven, CT
26 May 2023

37004518R00118